# HOMEGROWN
## BY FATHER & SON

JOHN & PIP BURTON-RACE

GROW AND COOK YOUR OWN FOOD

FORWARD BY RAYMOND BLANC OBE

**Homegrown by Father & Son**

By John & Pip Burton-Race



ISBN 978-0-9576556-2-1



A CIP catalogue record for this book is available from the British Library.

*Authors*
John Burton-Race, Pip Burton-Race

*Recipe editor*
Suzi Burton-Race

*Assistant chefs*
Harrison Brockington, Julien Picamil

*Photography*
Matt Austin, www.mattaustinimages.co.uk

*Editing, design and layout*
Andrew Chapman, www.preparetopublish.com

*Cover design*
Jon Ashford, www.jonashford.co.uk

*Public relations & digital marketing*
www.golbornenash.com

## SPECIAL ACKNOWLEDGEMENTS

Pip for having the idea; my wife Suzi for her editing prowess; Raymond Blanc for a lifelong friendship; Francis Yeoh for his incredible support; and for her devotion to the project, my agent, Helen Hokin.

## A BIG THANK YOU

Pip and I would like to acknowledge some very special people who not only believed in our project but generously supported it. These pages were brought to life thanks to every one of you.

Amanda Burden, Amelia Eyston, Andrew Walwyn, Angela Shine, Anita Delaney, Ann Tickner, Annie Parker Terblanche, Anthony Rew, Anthony Stevens, Bart Dudley, Bauston Wilde, Ben Davies, Ben Pavord, Brian Burden, Caroline Murray, Carrie Marks, Cat Barber, Catherine Ziemak, Charles Withers, Chris Murdoch, Chris Sherville, Damian Thornton, David Rai, David Smith, Dawn Dudley, Devon Sanner, Donny Cruce, Eleanor Dudley, Emma Wilson, Fariba Sutton, Francis Yeoh, Ian Fillis, Ian Toal, Jamie Rogers, Jilly Goolden, Jim Hall, John Philips, Jojo Szota, Jordan Wasserman, Julien Picamil, Kate Dudley, Kathy Murdoch, Katie Desautels, Liz Clark, L R Netherton, Maggie Cornhill, Marc Hevans, Marie Tkacik, Mark Harbour, Matthew Bond, Mike Shepherd, Oliver Dudley, Peter Green, Phil Knott, Rafiee Ghani, Raymond Blanc OBE, RK Alker, Roger Bullock, Ruth Yeoh, Sam Caldis, Samuel Maldonado, Stefan Pinter, Stephan Rauball, Stephen Humphries, Steven Byrne, Struan Coupar, Taylor Baird, Tim Wood and Wenny.

To join John Burton-Race's members' club visit **www.johnburtonrace.co.uk**, sign up and receive exclusive invitations, offers and discounts on future events and products.

# PIP's GROWING CALENDAR

What we grew. When we grew it. Our south-east-facing garden in South Devon is in one of the hottest parts of the UK and probably bears produce about a fortnight earlier than more northerly parts of the country.

| Key | |
|---|---|
| Plant | PLANT |
| Harvest | HARVEST |
| Plant & Harvest | PLANT & HARVEST |

| Produce | J | F | M | A | M | J | J | A | S | O | N | D |
|---|---|---|---|---|---|---|---|---|---|---|---|---|
| Broad Beans | | | Plant | Plant | | Harvest | Harvest | Harvest | | | | |
| Beetroot | | | Plant | Plant | Plant | Plant & Harvest | Harvest | Harvest | Harvest | | | |
| Broccoli, Purple Sprouting | | | Plant & Harvest | Plant & Harvest | | | | | | | | |
| Cabbage, Savoy | | | Plant | Plant & Harvest | Plant & Harvest | | | | | | | |
| Carrots | | | Plant | Plant | Plant & Harvest | Plant & Harvest | Plant & Harvest | Plant & Harvest | | | | |
| Cauli-flower | | | Plant | Plant & Harvest | Harvest | Harvest | Harvest | | | | | |
| Courgettes | | | | | Plant | | Harvest | Harvest | Harvest | | | |
| Cucumber | | | | | Plant | | Harvest | Harvest | Harvest | | | |
| Dwarf Beans | | | | Plant | Plant | Plant | Harvest | Harvest | Harvest | | | |
| French Dwarf Beans | | | | Plant | Plant | Plant | Harvest | Harvest | Harvest | | | |
| Garlic | | | Plant | Plant | | | Harvest | Harvest | | | | |
| Goose-berries | | | Plant | Plant | | | Harvest | Harvest | | | | |
| Leeks | | | Plant | Plant | | | | Harvest | Harvest | Harvest | Harvest | |
| Lettuce | | | Plant | Plant & Harvest | Plant & Harvest | Plant & Harvest | | | | | | |
| Marrow | | | | Plant | Plant | Harvest | Harvest | Harvest | | | | |
| Parsnips | | | Plant | Plant | Plant | | | | Harvest | Harvest | Harvest | Harvest |
| Peas | | | Plant | Plant & Harvest | Plant & Harvest | Plant & Harvest | Harvest | | | | | |
| Potatoes, Arran Pilot and Maris Piper | | | Plant | Plant | Plant & Harvest | Harvest | Harvest | | | | | |
| Radish | | | Plant | Plant & Harvest | Plant & Harvest | Plant & Harvest | Plant & Harvest | Harvest | | | | |
| Rasp-berries | | | Plant | Plant | | Harvest | Harvest | | | | | |
| Rhubarb | | Plant (Harvest in Year 2) | Plant (Harvest in Year 3) | | | | | | | | | |
| Spinach | | | Plant | Plant | Plant & Harvest | Plant & Harvest | Plant & Harvest | Harvest | Harvest | | | |
| Spring Onions | | Plant | Plant | Plant | Harvest | Harvest | Harvest | | | | | |
| Straw-berries | | | Plant | Plant | Harvest | Harvest | Harvest | | | | | |
| Swede | | | | Plant | Plant | Plant | Plant | | Harvest | Harvest | Harvest | Harvest |
| Tomatoes | | | Plant | Plant | | | Harvest | Harvest | Harvest | | | |
| Turnips | | | Plant | Plant | Plant & Harvest | Plant & Harvest | Plant & Harvest | Harvest | Harvest | | | |

# CONTENTS

# FOREWORD by Raymond Blanc OBE

When John Burton-Race, my protégé and great friend, told me he was digging a vegetable garden with his son Pip, I was filled with delight and enthusiasm for their project. And when, shortly after, he announced he was working on a batch of new recipes inspired by the produce they were growing, I was thrilled and offered an abundance of encouragement.

Then, one morning in late summer, John messaged me: he had started turning his food-growing adventures into a book and would I write the foreword? I texted straight back that it would be an honour.

For my whole life I have been a vocal and passionate advocate of growing one's own food. Travelling back in my mind to childhood, I am in the garden tending vegetables with my father. Together we are planting, nurturing and harvesting the season's offerings, ready to deliver to my mother in the kitchen. Brimming with ideas, she elevates our freshly culled herbs and vegetables into dishes I can still taste today.

Working the land together as a family, respecting the rhythm of the seasons, eating in easy conviviality together: the deep connections to homegrown food that I forged during those idyllic days inform everything I do at Le Manoir today.

I find in *Homegrown by Father & Son* a heartwarming reminder of my childhood. Here is John with his son Pip connecting to the land, connecting as a family, living sustainably, tending their new garden with love and respect and purity.

I stand in awe of young Pip, fully armoured in bee suit, collecting honey from his hives, or wading through the chicken coop before dawn to collect the morning eggs or up to his knees in manure to nourish his vegetable garden. Pip is learning to live by the seasons, as I did.

And I salute my great friend and chef extraordinaire, John Burton-Race, for bringing a new clutch of recipes into being. It has been too long coming. In their pared-back design, these family- and cost-friendly recipes are accessible to everyone, while being underpinned by all the rigour and experience of one of our country's greatest chefs.

Buying local, seasonal produce is critical for our health and for the environment. To go one step further and grow and cook your own food – whether a single tomato plant on a windowsill, a few herbs in a pot or a garden bursting with prize-winning marrows – is to show by your hands and heart that the health of your family and of the planet itself really matters.

I remember commenting to John once, many years ago, that fifty percent of a great dish is determined by the quality of its ingredients. For readers inspired to accept the challenge of growing and cooking your own food, I hope you will discover the truth of this for yourselves.

This unique and enchanting book urges us to reconnect with nature and one another, to learn the forgotten skills of gardening and to get cooking! It is a book after my own heart.

**Raymond Blanc OBE**
Oxfordshire, September 2020

# INTRODUCTION

This book was born out of lockdown on 23 March 2020.

Not long before then I had been working in Vietnam. Suddenly, at the end of January, I found myself on a flight home. As my plane took flight from a country already locking down, little did I know I was heading straight into the same scenario back home.

I immediately found a job in Villefranche-sur-Mer, then another in London and then a third near my home on the farm in Devon. One by one, as we became increasingly entrenched in the pandemic, the gigs got cancelled. No job and no money.

My son Pip suggested we plant a vegetable and fruit garden on a small piece of land next to the chicken run. Between us we cleared the ground, rotavated the soil and dug in some horse manure. After much discussion, Pip set off with great enthusiasm planting at least 20 different vegetables and several types of fruit. He was determined that this would get me out and about and my mind focused on something other than the morbid Covid.

It's interesting. I never thought of myself as a gardener but the project quickly got me hooked. Putting plants and seeds in the ground is surprisingly therapeutic and it was great for my relationship with Pip as together we surmounted the various obstacles involved in creating a vegetable garden.

Days passed when we didn't see a car on the lane. For the first time in eight years, we heard the rare but unmistakable song of the cuckoo. We witnessed the courting ritual of a greater spotted woodpecker which lasted at least a fortnight and, for the first time in Devon, we were humbled to see a magnificent red kite circling majestically above the house as if surveying our efforts to tend the garden.

The weather, the countryside, the walks, the sprightly aromas of spring evolving into balmy summer scents; all of it will always stay in my mind.

But back to the garden.

Pip, armed with books and the internet, literally immersed himself in the science of growing food. And the fact is, I think, just by growing up in rural Devon and everything that that involves, from being surrounded by rolling hills and chicken poo and horse manure and having really beautiful soil at our fingertips, he just made the produce burst into life in record time – much to the envy of some of our close gardening friends.

When I was living in France, some years ago, I created a cookery book inspired by the produce that that came in and out of season in the local markets. I took the reader through a whole year of seasonal French produce. So, we had the idea that for this book, I would create recipes out of the produce that Pip and I grew over the spring and summer months, which was effectively the duration of lockdown.

Now, the scope of the recipes in this book reaches beyond the ingredients we grew in our garden. But what we didn't grow ourselves either came from the chickens or the bees or was traded with locals for something that we did actually produce and thus the dishes were born. But not before trialling and testing each one three times.

A footnote to the above paragraph. Chocolate is the main ingredient in certain recipes in this book. A chocolate-free book is not a book. Chocolate got me through lockdown. If I could have grown it I would have. There are exceptions to every rule.

There is an irony in that one of the very few times we went to the supermarket during lockdown was not to buy food, but a little plastic greenhouse. A bargain at £45.00, it produced the nicest, juiciest cucumbers and tomatoes I have ever eaten. Sadly, the advent of Storm Francis in the last week of August saw Pip's beloved greenhouse lifted up and away into the clouds. It was last spotted in Scunthorpe.

We did have our failures; the rats took care of over half our cauliflowers. Who knew rats were partial to caulis? Our first carrots were a little suspect; I think the soil was off balance, and our purple sprouting broccoli was admittedly a bit feeble.

For that reason, scattered amongst my recipes are helpful little snippets of gardening advice. Pip's Tips were written by my son to help others avoid some of the pitfalls, trials and tribulations we went through. They are, undoubtedly, the book's secret sauce.

I'd like to finish with a warning about runner beans. We grew at least a ton and not on purpose, either. It was runner beans for lunch, runner beans for dinner and runner beans three ways every day for a fortnight. There are still hundreds of jars of the things I turned into chutney in our dry store. And even though everything we grew tasted miles better than anything you could ever buy, hand on heart I can say when it comes to runner beans, I am over and done with them. Now and forever.

This little book is designed to entertain and inspire others like us to plant and nurture and harvest and then cook simple, family dishes. It is impossible to explain the sheer anticipation and joy of watching a garden grow and a family come together to enjoy the fruits of their own labour.

A special thank you to my lifelong friend, and now fellow gardener, Raymond Blanc OBE for generously writing the foreword to this book. And to all the backers who made *Homegrown by Father & Son* a material reality. They are named, each and every one, in the backers' thank you list.

This book is for my son, Pip, and wife, Suzi; my family and lockdown companions. I could not have written it without them.

**John Burton-Race**
Devon

Sketch by Pip Burton-Race

# INTRODUCTION TO THE GARDEN

I wrote this book with my dad. For a long time I've wanted to produce my own food and Dad is obviously the perfect person to make meals out of what I grow. We spent the whole of lockdown, from March to summer, experimenting in the garden and the kitchen. We worked hard, ate loads and had a lot of fun.

I had to do a lot of background research and our family friend, Trevor, who is like an encyclopedia of gardening, gave me a head start. It's not until you've been through the whole growing cycle of a vegetable from planting the first seed to sticking your knife and fork in and eating it, that you can really find out what works and what doesn't.

I've written a series of tips based on what I found out working in the garden. They are scattered through the book as 'Pip's Tips' and hopefully will help you have growing success.

## My garden layout

I started out with just one small vegetable patch which was part of our chicken run. But gradually over the weeks, I persuaded Dad to keep clearing more of the land. More and more we cleared until eventually we ended up with a three-tiered sweep of garden that runs from the chicken houses at the top down to the first vegetable patch at the bottom.

### Bottom tier

This is the first patch we started, which was covered in weeds and grasses. We borrowed a rotavator from a neighbour, then Dad and I added some well-rotted horse manure to the garden and dug it in. It really improved the quality of the soil. Next, I planted potatoes, beetroot, peas, leeks, cauliflower, lettuce and a selection of herbs at the beginning of April.

### Middle tier

The soil here was much finer but quite stony and, as I found out, not suitable for deep-rooted vegetables. The carrots we first grew came out in weird shapes as they had to grow their way around the stones in the soil. Next time round, I planted them on the top tier with a much better result. I also planted another row of potatoes, runner beans, spring onions, cabbage and garlic. This was a remarkably successful patch of garden and the produce was really pleasing for a first attempt.

### Top tier

The years of chickens pooing in the garden have really helped the soil quality. It is excellent. Fine and naturally rich. This part was much easier to dig. I planted courgettes, strawberries, French beans, spinach, parsnips, raspberry canes, and more carrots. I even planted out some cucumbers from the greenhouse as the spring weather was so good.

This book includes spring and summer produce, tips and recipes. Homegrown Part 2 will be our next book covering autumn and winter, which we'll publish next year.

I never imagined at the start of lockdown we'd grow so much veg, write a book about it, do a photoshoot and make all sorts of business decisions to get the book published.

This is my first vegetable patch and my first book. Lockdown was challenging but, in other ways, it has been an awesome year.

**Pip Burton-Race**
Devon

# Pip's Picks

*family favourites*

# Asparagus Salad, Parma Ham with Honey & Red Wine Vinegar Dressing

*Serves 4*

For our first attempt at making a vegetable garden, I can say growing our own asparagus has been incredibly rewarding not to mention cost effective. We've always eaten so much of it in the short season from April to the end of May; stepping outside to gather it has been a joy.

**You will need**

20 large spears of asparagus

2 tbsp of olive oil

8 slices of Parma ham

2 eggs, boiled and grated

50g Parmesan cheese, for shaving

picked chervil sprigs (for garnish)

**For the dressing**

1 tsp Dijon mustard

1 tsp clear honey

1 tsp red wine vinegar

2-3 anchovy fillets, finely chopped

4 tbsp olive oil

1 garlic clove, chopped to a paste

milled black pepper

**Method**

1. Mix all the ingredients for the dressing together with a whisk. You should not need any salt as the anchovies have their own.
2. Keep aside.

**For the asparagus**

1. Cut off the woody ends of the asparagus and just down from the tip gently peel the spears.
2. Boil two eggs in a saucepan of water for five minutes. Remove them with a slotted spoon and refresh them in cold water. When cooled, peel off the shells.
3. Heat a large frying pan on the stove. Add the olive oil and fry the asparagus to colour, this takes just two minutes. Do not overcook them. Take them off the stove.
4. Lay the Parma ham with two slices overlapping each other on a tray or clean work surface. Place five asparagus spears on top and roll them so that they are completely wrapped in the ham. Place each asparagus onto your serving plates.
5. Drizzle a little of the dressing around the plates and grate some boiled egg on top. With a peeler shave 2-3 pieces of Parmesan and dress with a few sprigs of chervil. Serve.

# Courgette Flowers with Tomato & Mozzarella

*Serves 4*

**It is flaming June and the courgettes are beginning to flower. In England we do not use these delicate flowers for culinary purposes however in France, Spain, and Italy they are extremely popular. I like to use them as a floral pocket filled with a crab mousse, prawns and couscous or deep fried in a tempura batter. Just use your imagination. This dish is great for a summer lunch and will use up some of your early ripening tomatoes.**

**You will need for the tomato sauce**

6 ripe tomatoes

1 onion, finely chopped

2 garlic cloves, chopped to a paste

1 tsp tomato paste

1 sprig of thyme

**For the flowers**

choose 20 of your best courgette flowers picked on a dry day

250g mozzarella

1 bunch basil, chopped

1 lemon and zest

salt and black pepper

**Method**

1. With the point of a sharp knife cut out the core from the tomatoes and make small crosses at the top of each tomato. Put a pan, half filled with water, on the stove and bring to the boil. When boiling, plunge the tomatoes into the boiling water and leave them there for 10-15 seconds. Remove them with a slotted spoon and place in a bowl. Cool them immediately under cold running water. When cold, pour off the water. Place them on a clean tea towel to dry. With a small knife peel off the skin and discard.
2. Cut the tomatoes into quarters. Scoop out the pulp and seeds into a bowl and put the tomato flesh in another bowl.
3. Place a saucepan on the stove to heat. Add half the olive oil, and immediately add the finely chopped onions, garlic, and cook to soften, no colour. Stir in the tomato paste and add the tomato pulp. Place a lid on the pan and cook gently for about 20 minutes. This is the sauce.
4. When cooked, pour the tomato sauce into a sieve placed over a bowl and press the tomatoes with a wooden spoon trapping the residue. Discard.
5. Cut four pieces of the tomato flesh lengthways, each one sliced into three pieces and do the same for the mozzarella balls. Place on a plate to garnish the dish.
6. Dice the remaining tomato flesh and mozzarella and cover with chopped basil. Season with salt and milled black pepper and stir in a tablespoon of olive oil.
7. Pre-heat the oven 150C/Fan 130C/300F/Gas 2.
8. Carefully open the courgette flowers and remove the stamens. With a teaspoon fill each flower with the mozzarella stuffing. Place them in a flat oven dish. Pour the tomato sauce over and cook for about 10 minutes in the oven.

Serve with garlic bread or sprinkle with garlic croutons.

# Home Cured Hot Smoked Mackerel with Glazed Beetroot & Horseradish Cream

*Serves 4*

I love hot smoked fish. You can smoke salmon, cod and mackerel with a variety of flavoured wood chips such as cherry, hickory, oak and my favourite, apple.

**You will need**

4 medium sized mackerel, filleted and pin boned

50g salt

50g sugar

1 tbs olive oil

1.5lb bag of smoking chips

**Method**

You can get your fishmonger to prepare the mackerel for you but if not here is how.

1. To prepare the fish, gut them, cut off the heads and with a sharp knife carefully remove the first fillet slicing from top to tail one side of the backbone. This will expose the bone. Again, with a sharp knife slice underneath the bone, head to tail. Discard the fish frame.
2. Using some eyebrow tweezers pull out any pin bones which run down the middle of the fillets or carefully run the knife either side of the bloodline and pull out the pin bones in one strip.
3. Lay the mackerel fillets skin side up on an ovenproof tray.
4. Mix the salt and sugar together and sprinkle over the fish. Cover with cling film and place in the fridge for about 30 minutes. This is the curing process.
5. Remove the mackerel and wash off the salt and sugar with cold water. Dry the fillets with a clean kitchen cloth. When dry rub with olive oil.
6. Line an old roasting tin (not your best one) with foil and sprinkle the wood chips over the bottom of the tin to cover.
7. Lay a wire rack on top of the wood chips. Place the mackerel onto the rack and place another tray, lid, or foil on top. Make sure it fits tightly.
8. Place the tray over a medium heat until the chips begin to smoke. Your kitchen will smell beautifully smoky after this! Or you can smoke the fillets on a BBQ outside if you do not want the fire alarm to go off.
9. As soon as you see the smoke coming out of the sides of the lid turn off the heat and leave the mackerel to smoke for 10 minutes. You can move the tray outside to smoke if you prefer.
10. Lift the rack from the smoker. Turn a fillet over with the point of a knife. It should come away clean. If the fish is undercooked, place it in the oven for a few minutes to finish. Take the fish off the rack and peel off the skins. Place on a dish to cool. When cold refrigerate until required.

Sketch by Pip Burton-Race

**For the horseradish cream**

75ml double cream

½ lemon, juice of

2 tsp freshly grated horseradish

½ an apple, peeled and grated

a pinch of sugar

salt and milled black pepper

1 tbsp live natural yoghurt

**For the horseradish cream**

1. Put the grated apple and horseradish into a bowl and mix.
2. Stir in the lemon juice, sugar, salt, and pepper.
3. In a separate bowl lightly whip the cream and fold this into the horseradish mix,
4. Finally add the natural yoghurt.

I like to serve this dish with glazed beetroot (see page 120), potato and shallot salad with a classic French dressing (p29). Lay the mackerel fillets on top of the potato salad and glazed beetroot and spoon the horseradish cream over the fillets. Drizzle the remaining French dressing around the plate and sprinkle with chopped chives.

**PIP'S TIP**

## Beetroot

I started my beetroot off in the greenhouse and when we transferred them into the garden they were really, really thick with about five plants in one container (because one seed can produce up to 4 or 5 plants). When you transfer them into the garden, be sure you do not disturb the roots by pulling them apart and killing the plant. Be gentle.

# Pumpkin Risotto

## *Serves 6*

This is a lovely rich risotto. First, make a pumpkin puree; you can use a butternut squash if you prefer. I like to garnish this dish with a few sliced mushrooms; oyster or wild mushrooms are insanely good. Some truffle oil dotted over the finished risotto makes for an incredible finish.

**You will need for the puree**

1 litre white chicken stock
500g pumpkin, quartered
60g butter
50ml olive oil
2 garlic cloves, peeled
2 sprigs of thyme
2 sprigs of sage

**For the risotto**

2 tbs olive oil
2 shallots or onion, finely chopped
300g carnaroli or arborio rice
100ml dry white wine
100g Parmesan cheese
100g cold butter diced
1 tbs crème fraiche or ricotta

**Method for the puree**

1. Cut the pumpkin into quarters and remove the seeds. Clean off the seeds and put them on a separate tray to dry.
2. Pre-heat the oven to 160C/Fan 140C/325F/Gas 3.
3. Place the pumpkin in a roasting tray and cover with the butter, olive oil, thyme, and sage. Cover with foil and roast in the oven until tender but not coloured. This will take about 45 minutes.
4. When cooked, scrape out the flesh with a spoon into a food processor. Make sure you remove the thyme and sage sprigs and discard. Puree the pumpkin with the garlic until smooth. Scrape it out into a bowl to cool.
5. Heat the stock, you can use chicken or vegetable and bring to the boil.

**For the risotto**

1. Heat the olive oil in a large saucepan and fry the shallots to soften but not colour.
2. Add the rice and cook it until it becomes translucent.
3. Pour in the dry white wine, turn up the heat and stir the rice until the wine has fully evaporated.
4. A ladle at a time, add the hot stock stirring continuously.
5. Add all the stock. This process will take about 15 minutes. Once all the stock has been added check the rice, it should be tender but with a slight bite. The liquid should be thick, syrupy and bubbling. This is now a risotto.
6. Add 150g of the prepared pumpkin puree, stirring continuously, and add a piece of butter at a time to the risotto.
7. Stir in the remaining butter; this process will take about 5 minutes. Add the Parmesan and when fully incorporated stir in the crème fraiche. Check the seasoning, add salt and milled black pepper to taste.
8. If the risotto is too thick add a little more stock or a tablespoon of water. It must be syrupy and of a loose consistency.

Serve immediately. You can dry the seeds of the pumpkin in a warm oven sprinkled with soy sauce. Sprinkle a few of these on top of your risotto or serve with some mushrooms and a little rocket salad.

# Goat's Cheese, Sun-dried Cherry Tomato & Black Olive Tart

*Serves 4*

This is my go-to summer lunch eaten outside in the sunshine. I like it with a salad tossed in a walnut dressing which to take it to another level. To drink with it, I reach for a cheap and cheerful Muscadet or any light, crisp wine.

**You will need for the pastry**

75g butter
120g plain flour
25g Parmesan cheese, grated
1 egg yolk
pinch of salt
1 tbsp of cold water
18cm tart tin

**For the filling**

150g goat's cheese (soft and preferably made with raw milk)
50g Parmesan cheese, grated
1 egg
1 egg yolk
1 garlic clove, crushed to a paste
35ml double cream
25g black olives, pitted and cut in half
25g sun-dried cherry tomatoes
salt and milled black pepper
3-4 leaves of shredded basil

**Method**

1. Cut the butter into small cubes. Sieve the flour into a bowl and rub in the butter to resemble breadcrumbs. Add the salt and finely grated Parmesan cheese.
2. Add the egg yolk and a tablespoon of cold water. Bring the pastry together and gently roll it into a ball.
3. Dust a work surface with a little flour and roll out the pastry and line the tart tin. Put it in the fridge to cool, rest and set for about 20 minutes.
4. Place a circle of greaseproof paper down into the tart base and cover with baking beans or uncooked rice.
5. Bake in the oven at 190C/Fan 170C/375F/Gas 5 for about 15 minutes. Remove the contents when the tart case is cooked. Be careful as the beans or rice will be hot.

**For the filling**

1. In a bowl beat the goat's cheese to a small paste. Stir in the egg and egg yolk.
2. Season with salt and pepper and stir in the cream.
3. Fold in the grated Parmesan cheese.
4. Add the chopped olives and sun-dried tomatoes and shredded basil.
5. Pour the mixture into the blind baked tart case and bake for 20 minutes at 180C/Fan 160C/350F/Gas 4 or until golden.

**PIP'S TIP**

## Tomatoes

I made my own growbags from empty plastic horse feed bags filled with compost and manure. As the tomatoes grow, they send outside shoots that gobble up the precious nutrients that should be travelling to feed the fruit. Snap them off as soon as you can. Tomatoes thrive in rich, well-draining soil. Keep them hydrated and put a blanket of mulch at the root base to stop the water from evaporating. You can even add shredded bark to prevent the weeds and grass climbing up the plant.

# Field Mushroom Tagliatelle with Smoked Bacon & Parsley

*Serves 4*

**It's the beginning of September and the weather has been perfect for field mushrooms. We try to pick them early in the morning when they've just come up and optimistically bring a basket along as we're heading out with the dogs. It's all eyes on the ground to find these prized mushrooms with their rich, earthy flavour. Once picked, they keep for a day or two then the gills turn black and your mushroom sauce will take on a dark colour when cream or milk is added.**

**You will need**

200g smoked bacon, cut into lardons

2 garlic cloves, peeled and crushed

500g picked field mushroom, peeled, and sliced or good quality flat mushrooms

450g fresh or dried tagliatelle

1 tbsp olive oil

1 tbsp butter

1 large tbsp mascarpone

1 tbsp parsley, chopped

Parmesan cheese, grated to finish

truffle oil, drizzle of (optional)

milled black pepper and salt

**Method**

1. In a large frying pan heat the olive oil, add the bacon and fry to colour. With a slotted spoon remove the bacon and place in a bowl and set aside.
2. In the same pan, add the sliced mushrooms, garlic and butter and gently cook.
3. Meanwhile bring a large saucepan of salted water to the bowl and cook the fresh tagliatelle it will take only 3 minutes. If using dried tagliatelle this will take at least 10 minutes. When the pasta is tender but with a slight bite, strain through a colander and put the pasta in the pan with the mushrooms.
4. Now add the bacon lardons, mascarpone and mix all the ingredients gently with a wooden spoon.
5. Sprinkle with chopped parsley.
6. Divide the tagliatelle into four bowls and top the dish with Parmesan cheese and sprinkle with a little truffle oil.

**PIP'S TIP**

## Seedlings

When you are watering seedlings, try to use tap water rather than rain water, which has high acidity and may damage the young plants.

# Crab Claws with Mayonnaise and Homemade Bread

One of the nicest crustaceans found around the Devon coastline is the spider crab. In Spain and France, they are highly prized and command a good price in the markets. To be fair, they look a bit odd and maybe that's why not a lot of people want them here. The other day our friendly fishermen rocked up out of the blue armed with a carrier bag full of them. We fired up the Calor Gas burner outside and filled a large cooking pot of water, throwing in a handful of salt. The minute it came to the boil we lobbed in the crab and 10 minutes later they were cooked. We cracked open the claws with a hammer and dived in with some homemade mayonnaise using lobster picks to extract the good bits.

# Homemade Mayonnaise

### *Makes 500ml*

I do not know what it is in this house but both Suzi and Pip eat copious amounts of this stuff. It seems to get dolloped on most things. My favourite is egg and watercress sandwiches. However, it is handy to make your own and a lot better than any you can buy. It can be used as a foundation for several different sauces all through the seasons. For example, tartare sauce for your fish and chips, cocktail sauce for your prawns, crab and lobster, and as a base for a Caesar salad.

**You will need**

3 egg yolks

1 dstsp French mustard (Beaune or Dijon will do)

200ml sunflower oil

200ml Light olive oil

¼ of lemon, juice of

1 tbsp of white wine vinegar

1 tsp sugar, gently warmed in a pan to dissolve

Salt and ground white pepper to taste

**Method**

The white wine vinegar and sugar combined is called a gastric – sweet and sour, it will bring out the flavour of the sauce.

1. Place the egg yolks in a bowl, set at a medium speed and whisk until light, fluffy and pale in colour. Stop whisking and add the mustard.
2. Continue whisking at a gentle speed and add the oil at a continuous stream. The mayonnaise will start to thicken, add the lemon juice, vinegar and sugar (gastric).
3. Continue to add the oil. If the mayonnaise gets to thick sprinkle in a little warm water and continue mixing.
4. Season with a little salt and ground white pepper.

Put the finished mayonnaise into a clean jar with a spatula and keep in the fridge with a tight lid on. It should keep for several days.

# Spaetzle Dumplings with Pesto

*Serves 4*

**Everyone's pasta-making mad now and I completely understand why. Sometimes, you want the result but haven't got the time. Spaetzli provide the perfect pasta quick-fix and a great accompaniment to this simple basil pesto.**

**You will need**

120g plain flour
1 tsp ground nutmeg
pinch of salt
milled black pepper
1 tbsp parsley, chopped
3 eggs, beaten
60ml milk

**For the pesto**

75g basil leaves
60g pecorino or Parmesan cheese cut into small pieces
60g pine nuts
3 cloves garlic
125ml olive oil

**Method**

1. Sieve the flour into a large bowl and add the nutmeg, salt, and pepper.
2. Whisk the eggs and milk together and pour the mixture into a jug. Gradually pour the mixture into the flour whisking constantly until all the liquid is incorporated into the flour. It should resemble a thick batter.
3. Place a large pan on the stove half filled with boiling water. Put a colander on top and with a ladle push half the batter through the colander. The batter will fall to the bottom of the pan. Use a slotted spoon as it floats to the surface to scoop it out. Immediately place it into iced cold water in a bowl. Repeat this process for the other half to make the pasta.
4. When the pasta is cold, drain it off and lay it onto a clean kitchen towel. Transfer to a tray and refrigerate until needed.
5. To re-heat the pasta, melt 30g of butter in a frying pan. Add the pasta and cook in foaming butter for 2 minutes. Season with a little salt and pepper.

**For the pesto**

1. Place the basil leaves, cheese and garlic into a food processor. Add the pine nuts and whizz to a paste or crumb.
2. While the blades are still moving pour in the olive oil to create a creamy sauce.

# Minced Lamb, Flat Bread & Ricotta

*Serves 6*

A friend of mine farms Dorper sheep, which originated from the Blackhead Persian crossed with a Dorset Horn. Their meat is sublime. This recipe makes 2 large flat breads or 6 smaller ones. As an alternative to ricotta I might use a soft goat's cheese mixed with 1 tablespoon of olive oil to a paste. This is a family favourite supper devoured al fresco on a hot summer evening. I like to serve this with Tomato, Cucumber, Red Onion and Feta Salad (recipe on p37).

**You will need for the flat bread dough**

450g strong white flour
20g fresh yeast or 2 tbsp of dried yeast
300ml lukewarm water
1 tsp salt
1 tsp sugar
2 tbsp olive oil

**For the minced lamb topping**

2 tbsp olive oil
2 onions, finely chopped
450g minced lamb
3 garlic cloves, peeled and crushed to a paste
2 large tomatoes, peeled, deseeded and finely chopped
1 tsp salt
1 tsp black pepper
1 tsp sugar
1 lemon, juice of
1 dstsp tomato paste
1 large bunch of flat leaf parsley, picked and finely chopped
250g ricotta cheese or soft goats' cheese
1 tsp toasted cumin seed
2 red chillies, deseeded and chopped finely
1 tsp sumac

**Method**

1. Pour 100ml of the lukewarm water into a bowl, add the sugar and stir in the yeast. Leave it for 5 minutes to activate.
2. Pour the activated yeast mixture into a food processor mixing bowl fitted with a dough hook attachment. Add all the remaining ingredients and 1 tablespoon of olive oil and mix well for about 10 minutes on a slow speed.
3. Turn the dough out onto a floured surface and knead it until it becomes elastic. Grease another bowl with the remaining olive oil, transfer the dough and cover it with a cloth. Place it in a warm part of your kitchen, the ideal temperature is about 24C. Leave for at least 2 hours to prove.

**For the minced lamb**

1. Heat a large frying pan on the stove. Add the oil and cook the onion and garlic until soft, it takes about 3 minutes. Immediately, add the minced lamb and fry to colour.
2. Add the tomatoes, salt, pepper, and sugar. Add the lemon juice and tomato paste. Cook for a further 10 minutes.
3. Drain off the lamb through a colander over a bowl to remove all the servicing fats and return the lamb to the pan with the heat turned off.
4. Stir in half the parsley and chopped chilli and set aside to cool.
5. Pre-heat the oven to 240C/Fan 220C/475F/Gas 9 with the trays in it. They must be hot.
6. When the dough has risen knead it again on a floured surface. Cut it into two and roll out one of the halves. Top the dough with half the lamb mince mixture and ricotta. Sprinkle with sumac. Remove one of the trays, drizzle it with olive oil and quickly place the flat bread down on it. It will take 9 minutes to cook and crisp.
7. Repeat this process for the other flat bread.

I like to serve this with a little more chopped parsley and a squeeze of lemon.

## Wool

If you live in a farming community, you might ask a sheep farmer to give you some unwanted fleece after shearing. Place it around root vegetables; it keeps in moisture and slugs will not crawl on the wool.

**PIP'S TIP**

# Garden Soups & Salads

*meals in one*

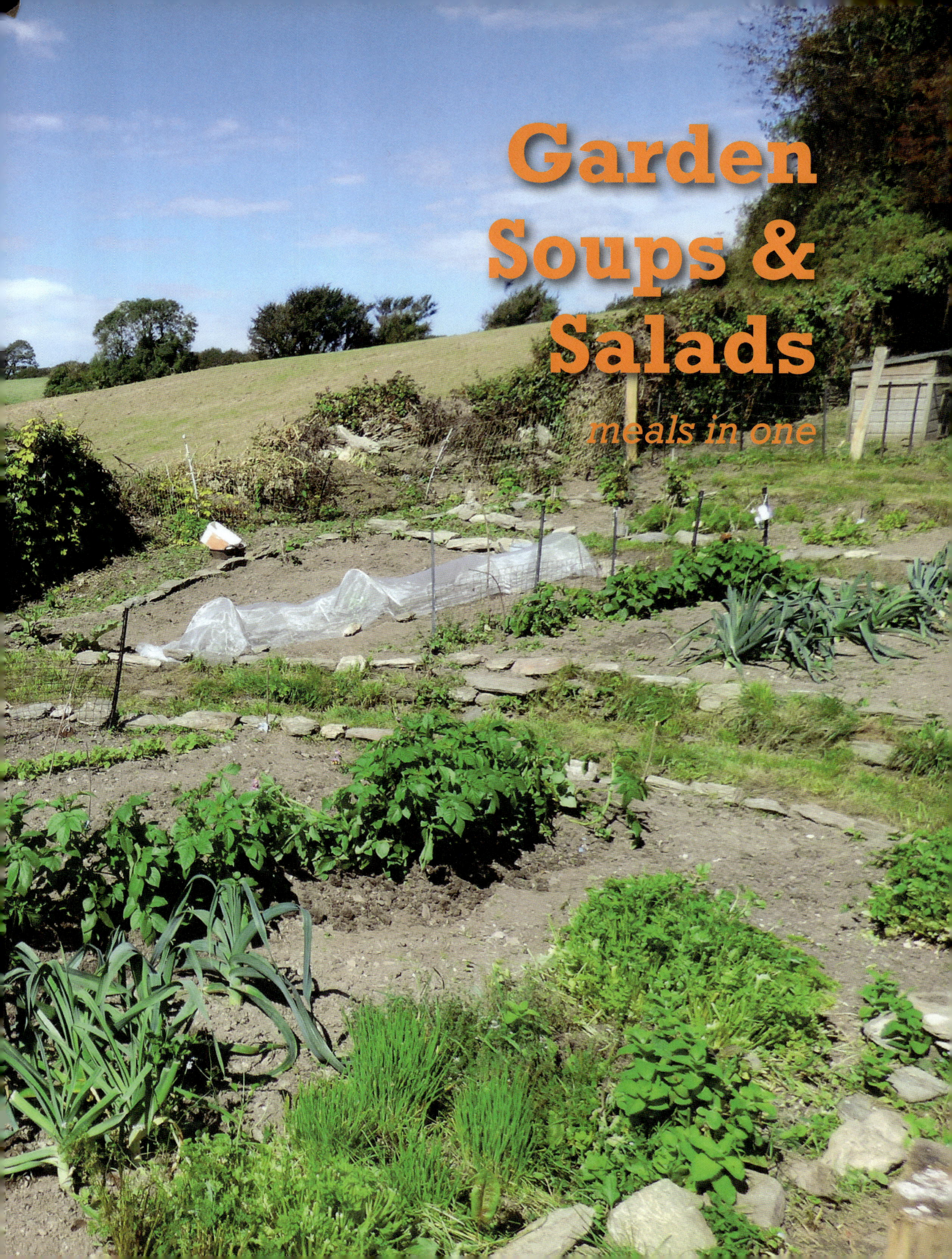

# Garden Soups & Salads

*meals in one*

# Potato & Shallot Salad with Classic French Dressing

*Serves 4*

Pip planted our potatoes in the spring after giving the potato beds a good going over with manure. They were remarkably successful. Come early summer our first crop was ready to pull. There is nothing quite like the taste of new potatoes. But dug fresh from your garden, for the first time ever? Priceless.

**You will need**

250g potatoes, new potatoes are best
1 shallot, peeled and finely sliced
2 hard-boiled eggs, shelled and grated
1 tbsp flat leaf parsley, chopped
2 tbsp of French dressing

**Method**

1. Bring a pan of salted water to the boil add the potatoes in their skins and cook for about 10 minutes or until tender. Drain and place them in a bowl to cool.
2. Once the potatoes are cool enough to touch, peel off their skins.
3. Bring another pan of water to the boil and boil the eggs for 5 minutes. Refresh in cold water until cooled and then peel.
4. Slice the potatoes, add the chopped shallots, and mix.
5. Chop the boiled eggs and add to the mixture.
6. Add the French dressing and mix.
7. Finally sprinkle with chopped parsley and serve.

## Potatoes

**PIP'S TIP**

I grew Maris Pipers and Arran Pilots. Just remember to keep banking them to protect the young potatoes from the light and frost damage. The light will turn the potatoes green and inedible. It's important to keep watering them in dry conditions.

# Warm Runner & Flageolet Bean Salad with Tomatoes & Garlic

*Serves 4*

**I've mentioned elsewhere on these pages my thoughts on runner beans. In peak season, triffid-like amounts kept emerging from the garden. On and on, they kept coming. It was bordering on an invasion. Still, what a great excuse to give homegrown food to neighbours and friends. My recipe is guaranteed to get any grower through their own fantastic runner bean crop. With fresh garlic from the garden and tomatoes from the greenhouse, I serve it warm on its own or with any lamb dish.**

**You will need**

225g flageolet beans

1 tbsp olive oil

25g butter

1 onion, finely chopped

2 garlic cloves, peeled and crushed

4 medium sized tomatoes, skinned, deseeded, and chopped

350g runner beans, prepared and finely sliced

150ml dry white wine

150ml vegetable or chicken stock

2 tbsp parsley, chopped

salt and black pepper milled

**Method**

1. Place the flageolet beans in a large pan covered with cold water and bring to the boil. Skim off any surfacing impurities and discard. Turn the heat down to a simmer and cook until tender. This takes about 1 hour.
2. Strain the beans into a colander and set aside.
3. In large frying pan heat the oil. Add the butter and fry the onions and garlic to soften but with no colour. Add the tomatoes and gently cooked for a further 2 minutes.
4. Add the flageolet beans, then add the runner beans and stir in the white wine and bring to the boil. Add the stock and stir.
5. Cover the pan with a lid and simmer for a few minutes until the runner beans are tender.
6. Finally turn up the heat to reduce the liquid in the pan to a glaze. Then sprinkle with the chopped parsley and season with salt and milled black pepper. Serve warm.

**PIP'S TIP**

## Runner beans

To speed up the germination I put the seeds in water for a few days. Be careful growing runner beans, they take on a life of their own. No matter how conservative you are, you will end up with more than you want or need!

Instead of using the correct bamboo canes to hold our plants up, I used hazel sticks as I could not access bamboo canes in the lockdown. At first they worked well but once the wind got up the weight of the plants was a recipe for disaster. As a first-time gardener mistakes will happen. However, I did rescue most of the beans by tying the sticks with string to some trees surrounding the garden for support. Next year I will use strong bamboo canes.

# Prawn, Haricot Bean & Parma Ham Salad with a Balsamic Dressing

*Serves 4*

**Fresh prawns are best and ideally with the last bit of the tail still on. Lemon zest and paprika add an extra dimension to this otherwise simple salad and make the whole dish sing.**

**You will need for the beans**

400g of haricot beans, semi dried

2 large carrots, peeled and left whole

2 large onions, peeled

4 cloves (2 pressed into each onion)

3 garlic cloves, peeled

1 bay leaf

water to cover

**For the salad**

2 medium tomatoes, skinned and diced

350g large fresh prawns

150g Parma ham

1 unwaxed lemon, zest of

50g butter

2 tbsp of chicken stock

1 onion, peeled and finely chopped

1 clove of garlic, peeled and finely chopped

pinch of paprika

**For the dressing**

2 tbsp olive oil

1 tbsp sherry vinegar

1 dstsp of balsamic vinegar

salt and pepper

1 tbsp chopped parsley

**Method for the beans**

1. Soak the beans overnight in a bowl of cold water.
2. Strain the beans and place them in a large saucepan. Add the peeled whole carrots, onions studded with the cloves, garlic, and bay leaf. Cover with cold water and bring to the boil. With a ladle remove the surfacing impurities and discard. Turn down the pan to a gentle simmer; this should take about 40 minutes until tender.
3. Strain the beans and remove the onions, carrots and bay leaf then place in a bowl to cool and set aside. Reserve one carrot for later.

**For the salad**

1. Place a small pan of water on the stove to boil. Once the water comes to the boil, scald the tomatoes for about 20 seconds. Remove and refresh in cold water.
2. Remove the skin and cut them into quarters. Cut out the seeds and dice the flesh ½ cm square. Place them in a bowl.
3. Take the reserved carrot and dice as for the tomatoes then add to the tomato mixture.
4. Add the lemon zest to the tomato mix and stir.
5. Add the cooled beans to the tomatoes and stir in the finely chopped onion.
6. Heat a frying pan on the stove. Add the butter and crushed, chopped garlic. Add the prawns and sprinkle with paprika and sauté for 2 minutes. When coloured add the chicken stock to deglaze the pan then immediately pour the prawns into the bean salad.
7. Next rip the Parma ham into pieces and gently fold into the bean salad.

**For the dressing**

1. In a small bowl mix the olive oil, sherry vinegar and balsamic. Season with salt and pepper and pour over the bean salad.
2. Sprinkle with chopped parsley and spoon the salad into 4 small serving boils. Serve.

# Cucumber Salad with Mint, Flat Leaf Parsley, Chilli & Crème Fraiche

### *Serves 4*

It is Pip's first attempt at growing cucumbers and although they are not noticeably big their flavour is outstanding. The intensity of flavour you get from homegrown cucumbers makes this dish an excellent stand-alone. I might add, though, it is a belting accompaniment to a grilled steak.

**You will need**

2 cucumbers, medium sized

1 shallot, finely chopped

a small bunch of fresh mint, picked and chopped

a small bunch of flat leaf parsley, chopped

1 red chilli, deseeded and chopped

1 garlic clove, peeled and chopped finely

1 tsp of sugar

½ tsp of salt

½ lemon, juice of

1 tbsp white wine vinegar

1 tbsp mayonnaise

1 tbsp of crème fraiche

black pepper, lots of

**Method**

1. Peel the cucumbers and split them down the middle. With the point of a teaspoon scrape out the seeds and discard.
2. Cut the cucumbers in half and slice them as thinly as possible with a sharp knife. Put the sliced cucumber on a tray lined with a clean dry tea towel – they will give out a lot of water. When dry pick up the cloth and pour the cucumbers into a bowl.
3. Add the finely chopped shallots, mint, garlic and parsley. Top and tail a large red chilli, cut it in half and deseed. Chop it finely and add it to the cucumber.
4. Add the sugar, salt, lemon juice and white wine vinegar.
5. Stir in the mayonnaise and a large tablespoon of crème fraiche.
6. Season with lots of milled black pepper. Cover the bowl and refrigerate until required.

**PIP'S TIP**

## Cucumber

I decided to plant the climbing kind of cucumber so first I had to put up a trellis. They prefer to grow upwards and it keeps the cucumber off the damp ground where it is likely to rot. Not to mention the rats we have running around the chicken coop would eat the cucumbers if they could get into the greenhouse, which is out of bounds to rats.

## Mint

Wild mint takes over the garden. Ours started off growing around the borders of the veg garden but now it has worked its way into the garden itself. It basically has a mind of its own.

# Crab Soup with Rouille & Garlic Croutons

*Serves 8*

**We are obsessed with anything made from crab at home, but especially this soup. The first time I made it using Pip's garlic, boy did it pack a punch. What a difference.**

**You will need**

2kg crab shells
100ml olive oil
2 onions, peeled and chopped
1 carrot, peeled and chopped
2 sticks celery, chopped
1 bulb of fennel, chopped
1 bay leaf
1 sprig fresh tarragon
bunch of parsley stalks
1 sprig thyme
1 whole head of garlic cut in half
150g tomato paste
1 tin of chopped tomatoes
1 whole red pepper, deseeded and chopped
1 fresh chilli, chopped
4 tbsp of cognac
200ml white wine
2 litres of fish stock or 2 litres of water
½ a dozen white fish frames from the fish monger preferably sea bass
salt
1 lemon, juice of
250ml double cream
Gruyère cheese to sprinkle

**For the rouille**

2 large potatoes in their skins
2 garlic cloves, smashed to a puree
1 pinch saffron strands or powder
2 tbsp of tomato ketchup
2 egg yolks
100ml sunflower oil
100ml olive oil
1 dstsp water
salt and lemon juice

**Method**

1. Put a large pan on the stove or you can use a stock pot. When the pan is hot add the oil and as soon as it starts to smoke add the crab shells. Cook for about 10 minutes stirring to stop the shells from burning.
2. Add all the chopped vegetables, herbs and garlic while stirring continuously cook for a further 10 minutes.
3. Stir in the tomato paste but be careful not to let it burn on the bottom of the pan, so keep it moving.
4. Flambé the cognac and then add the white wine. Bring to the boil and then add the tinned tomatoes. Continue boiling and stirring the crab shells.
5. Add the fish stock or water and chopped washed fish frames. White flat fish bones are the best or a few sea bass frames.
6. Bring the soup to the boil and with a ladle skim off all the surfacing impurities and discard. Turn the heat down and allow the soup to cook for at least 1½ hours at a gentle simmer.
7. Taste the soup and add the salt and lemon juice then strain through a colander into another pan pushing the contents with a wooden spoon to force the liquid through. Discard the shells etc.
8. Now bring the soup back to the boil and again remove any surfacing impurities. Turn the heat down and continue to reduce the volume and thicken the soup. This takes about ½ an hour.
9. Whisk in the double cream and bring the soup back to the boil, then remove from the heat and strain it through a fine sieve into another pan or bowl. Reserve until required.

**For the rouille**

1. Bake the potatoes in the oven at 160C/Fan 140C/325F/Gas 3 for about 45 minutes until the skins are crispy but the potato is soft inside.
2. When the potatoes are cooled cut then in half lengthways and, with a spoon, scrape out the cooked potato into a bowl.
3. In a mixing bowl add the egg yolks and a dessert spoon of water and whisk it until the yolks become fluffy and pale in colour.
4. Mix the oils together in a jug and slowly drizzle the oil into the egg yolks whisking on a fast speed. When the oil has emulsified add the lemon juice, tomato ketchup and saffron then add the garlic paste. Check the seasoning, add a little salt and pepper to taste.
5. Carefully stir the mixture into the soft potato and mix until smooth. Reserve in a small bowl until needed

To serve the soup, firstly spoon the rouille into a soup bowl, then ladle the soup on top. Sprinkle the soup with crispy garlic croutons and finely grated Gruyère cheese.

See page 46 for Crispy Garlic Croutons recipe.

# Pea, Mint & Crème Fraiche Soup

*Serves 4-6*

Spring has been ridiculously hot and the vegetable garden is thriving. The only thing more satisfying than the abundance of peas we had is sitting in the sun and shelling them. I love peas. The sweet, delicate taste of the first crop is exquisite.

**You will need**

2kg peas in their pods (or 1kg frozen peas)
50g butter
1 shallot or small onion, peeled and chopped
1 garlic clove, peeled and chopped
1 sprig of fresh thyme
2 sprigs of fresh mint
450ml white chicken stock
250ml crème fraiche
salt and pepper
1 tsp of lemon juice

**Method**

1. Shell the peas. Melt the butter in a saucepan add the shallot and garlic and cook gently until softened.
2. Add the sprigs of thyme and mint and pour in the chicken stock. Bring the liquid to the boil and stir in the crème fraiche. Turn down the temperature to a simmer and cook for 10 minutes.
3. Remove the sprigs of thyme and mint and discard. Pour the liquid into a liquidiser and blend until smooth. Strain the soup into another saucepan, season with salt and pepper and a little lemon juice. Bring it back to the boil and serve.

If you serve this soup as a starter to a three-course meal, drizzle a little truffle oil over the top and sprinkle with a few chopped chives.

Or for something more substantial you can drop a poached bantam egg or a couple of soft poached quail's eggs into the bowl of soup at the last minute.

# Tomato, Cucumber, Red Onion & Feta Salad with a Mustard Dressing

*Serves 6*

**In April, Pip purchased a cheap greenhouse and planted a variety of seeds. We got a bumper crop of tomatoes and cucumbers which, with Pip's magic touch, appear quite easy to grow. Such a fresh and vibrant summer salad as this is great all on its own.**

**For the mustard dressing**

1 garlic clove, peeled and crushed

½ lemon, juice of

1 tsp sugar

60ml cider vinegar or white wine vinegar

salt and milled black pepper

1 dessert spoon Dijon mustard

150ml olive oil

100ml sunflower oil

**For the salad**

2 large tomatoes, cut into quarters and then in half again

½ cucumber, peeled, deseeded, and diced

1 red onion, chopped

1 tsp sugar

1 tsp salt

milled black pepper to taste

1 small tin of anchovies in olive oil

100g artichoke hearts in sunflower oil

100g feta cheese, crumbled

7- 8 basil leaves, ripped

5- 6 mint leaves, finely shredded

2 tbsp of the mustard dressing

100g French beans, topped, tailed, and blanched in boiling water

**Method for the dressing**

1. Whisk all the ingredients in a bowl. Taste for seasoning and transfer it into a bottle or Kilner jar with a tight-fitting lid. It will keep for two weeks.

**For the salad**

1. Cut the tomatoes into quarters and cut each quarter in half again. Place in a bowl.
2. Peel the cucumber and cut it into four pieces lengthways. With a small knife cut away the seeds and discard. Cut the cucumber into small dice and add them to the bowl.
3. Cut the red onion into small dice, fingernail size and add the anchovies in olive oil to the bowl.
4. Peel, crush and chop the garlic and add the ripped fresh basil leaves.
5. Add the sugar and seasonings.
6. Add the artichokes, allow 2-3 pieces per person.
7. Crumble the feta into small pieces and sprinkle on top of the salad then add the shredded mint leaves.
8. Bind the salad together with the mustard dressing and mix gently. Transfer the salad to your presentation dish.

# Cream of Cauliflower Soup with Truffle Oil

*Serves 4*

Ever since Pip was a little boy he has loved this soup, so planting his own cauliflowers was inevitable. Even though the first crop was eaten by rodents thought most likely to be rats, the second time around was an out-and-out success and I made this soup more than once in the season with Pip's very fine crop of large cauliflowers.

**You will need**

500g cauliflower
100g butter
1 onion, peeled and chopped
2 garlic cloves, peeled and crushed
1 sprig of fresh thyme
1 bay leaf
400ml whole milk
400ml white chicken stock
salt and pepper
truffle oil
50g butter, diced
50ml of double cream to finish
lemon, squeeze of to taste

**Method**

1. Trim, wash and cut the cauliflower into pieces. You can use the stalk immediately surrounding the flower.
2. In a large pan melt the butter and gently cook the cauliflower on a low heat for about 10 minutes.
3. Add the onions, garlic, thyme, and bay leaf to the cauliflower. Stir, then cover with a lid and cook for a further 5 minutes.
4. In another pan, heat the milk and chicken stock together. As soon as it boils, pour it over the cauliflower. Turn up the heat and cook the soup on a rapid simmer for ½ an hour or until the cauliflower is soft.
5. Add the seasoning then take the pan off the stove and pour in two stages, the soup into a liquidiser and blend smooth.
6. Strain the soup through a fine sieve into another pan. Bring the soup back to the boil stirring all the time. Do not let it catch on the bottom!
7. Whisk in the cream and add the diced butter and stir into the soup. Give the soup a taste. It may need a squeeze of lemon juice as some cauliflowers can be rather sweet.
8. Whisk the soup with a hand blender until it froths and ladle it into soup bowls. Drizzle a little truffle oil over the top and serve.

**PIP'S TIP**

## Cauliflower

A simple but effective trick is to fold the leaves around the developing head to keep it nice and white and protect it from mottling.

# Spiced Parsnip Soup with Parsnip Crisps

## *Serves 6*

Parsnips are probably my favourite vegetable. Roasted with honey and chilli with a Sunday roast they take a lot of beating. Our parsnips were planted as seeds outdoors in April and flourished in the warm soil. All being well, they will be ready to harvest in the autumn from September onwards.

**You will need**

500g parsnips, peeled and chopped

2 onions, chopped

2 garlic cloves, peeled and crushed

1 granny smith apple, cored and chopped

2-3 kaffir lime leaves

1 red chilli, chopped

1 dstsp medium curry powder

1 tsp cumin seed, 1/2 teaspoon turmeric

2-3 cardamom pods

50ml sunflower oil

50g butter

400ml white chicken stock

400ml coconut milk

salt and pepper, to taste

lemon juice, squeeze of

50ml double cream, to finish

1 bunch chives, chopped

**For the parsnip crisps**

3 medium sized parsnips

500ml sunflower oil for frying

**Method for the soup**

1. Peel, and chop the parsnips. Place a large pan on the stove to heat and add the oil and butter. Add the parsnips and gently cook and stir for about 10 minutes.
2. Add the chopped onions, garlic and diced apple and continue cooking.
3. Add all the spices and cook and stirring continuously for about 5 minutes.
4. In a separate pan bring the chicken stock to the boil and immediately pour it over the parsnips and stir.
5. Add the coconut milk and bring the soup to the boil. Skim off any surfacing impurities with a ladle and discard. Turn down the heat to a simmer and cook the soup for a further 40 minutes, stirring occasionally.
6. Season with salt and pepper and a squeeze of lemon juice and remove the soup from the stove.
7. Pour the soup, in two stages, into a liquidiser and mix until smooth. Pour the soup into a sieve over another pan. Repeat the process for the second batch.
8. Bring the soup to boil then stir in a little cream. To serve ladle the soup into the bowls and sprinkle with a few chopped chives and top with the parsnip crisps at the last minute or serve the crisps separately.

**For the parsnip crisps**

1. Pour the oil, a third of the way into a large saucepan and heat to 140C. The temperature must not be any higher or the crisps will burn due to the high sugar content in the parsnips.
2. Top, tail and peel the parsnips, and with a peeler from the top to bottom peel the parsnips into long thin ribbons.
3. When the oil has reached the temperature, fry a little too colour to golden brown. Move the crisps around in the oil for an even colour.
4. Remove the crisps to a tray covered with a layer of greaseproof paper. Repeat this process a few at a time for the remaining crisps.

# Pumpkin Soup, Oyster Mushrooms & Roasted Pumpkin Seeds

## *Serves 6*

This versatile vegetable is so much more than a Halloween lantern. I've turned its creamy flesh into soups, pies, curries, muffins... and that's just for starters. That said, come 31 October you'll always find a carved pumpkin lighting up the porch at home. For this recipe you can substitute the pumpkin for a butternut squash depending on what you've grown. Or bought!

**You will need**

1 medium sized pumpkin or a large butternut squash, cut into quarters

3 garlic cloves, peeled and crushed

2 sprigs of thyme

6 sage leaves

50ml olive oil

120g butter

1 glass dry white wine (125ml)

800ml chicken stock

60g Parmesan cheese, grated

125ml double cream

salt and milled white pepper

handful of fresh oyster mushrooms

1 tbsp of dried pumpkin seeds (optional)

**Method**

1. Cut the pumpkin or butternut squash into four and scrape out the seeds. (Keep the seeds for drying.) Place it in a roasting tray sprinkled with olive oil. Add the garlic and the sprigs of thyme and the sage leaves then cover the roasting pan with tin foil. Roast in the oven at 180C/Fan 160C/350F/Gas 4 for about 45 minutes.
2. When cooked take out the pumpkin and remove the foil. As soon as it is cool enough, scrape out all the flesh into a large saucepan. Add half (60g) of butter and cook on the stove over a medium heat, stirring occasionally. Add the dry white wine and continue to cook for about 5 minutes.
3. Stir in the grated Parmesan, add the chicken stock, and bring the soup to the boil. Skim off all the surfacing impurities and foam with a ladle and discard. Turn down the temperature and cook it on a fast simmer for about 15 minutes.
4. Add the cream and the remaining butter (60g). Season with salt and milled white pepper to taste.
5. Blend the soup in a liquidiser and strain it through a fine sieve into another pan. Keep warm.
6. Heat a small frying pan. Pick over the oyster mushrooms and cut off the end stalks. Add a little more olive oil to the pan and fry them to colour.

**To serve**

Ladle the soup into the bowls. Top each with a few mushrooms and toasted pumpkin seeds sprinkled on top. You can drizzle a little truffle or basil oil for more flavour. Small crispy croutons give the soup texture and small Parmesan dice dropped into the hot soup give an extra richness.

# English Onion Soup with Cornish Yarg Croutons

*Serves 4*

So rich and unctuous, this soup is a meal in itself. There is no better way to warm your soul than a hearty bowl of this soup.

**You will need for the soup**

3 tbsp of sunflower oil

5 large brown onions, peeled and finely chopped

50g butter

2 garlic cloves, peeled and finely chopped

1 bay leaf

1 rasher of smoked streaky bacon

2 sprigs of thyme

salt and milled black pepper

100ml dry sherry

100ml dry white wine

200ml beef stock or brown chicken stock

**For the croutons**

2 slices of homemade bread or good quality purchased bread cut into four

olive oil

sea salt

150g Cornish Yarg or Cheddar or Lancashire cheese

**Method**

1. Heat the oil in a large saucepan until it starts to smoke. Add the onions and butter and cook two caramelise but not burn. Add the rasher of smoked bacon.
2. Stirring frequently add the garlic, bay leaf and thyme. Cook for about 20 minutes. Season with salt and milled black pepper.
3. Add the sherry and boil to reduce by half of its original volume. Pour in the wine and do the same.
4. Pre-heat the oven to 180C/Fan 160C/350F/Gas 4 or grill.
5. Pour in the stock and bring the soup to the boil. With a small ladle carefully remove the surfacing fat and impurities and discard. Turn down the soup to a simmer and cook for a further 20 minutes.
6. Slice the bread into ½ cm thick slices and place them on a tray. Sprinkle with a little olive oil and toast them on both sides under the grill or roast in the oven until lightly golden. Remove the croutons and top them with the cheese.
7. Pour the finished soup into four soup bowls. Return the croutons to the grill to melt the cheese and place 2-3 on top of the hot soup. Serve immediately.

**PIP'S TIP**

## Fending off slugs

A jam jar with a drop of beer in the bottom is irresistible to slugs who slide their way inside, drink the beer and die. Do not use slug pellets ever. They will harm the precious hedgehog and other garden friends.

## Rotating the land

Potatoes are brilliant, they fight their way through all sort of nasties. They will keep the weeds at bay, which is great for planting the next vegetable crop. Remember where you planted your vegetables and rotate to prevent bugs and disease building up.

# A Simple Farmhouse Loaf

## *Makes 3 loaves*

We've become a nation of bakers and breadmakers. But just in case you haven't got on board with the movement yet, you could do worse than start with this recipe. It's so simple, I recommend you give it a go.

**You will need**

750g plain unbleached bread flour

600ml lukewarm water

25g fresh yeast

15g salt

**Method**

1. Place the flour in the bowl of an electric mixer with a dough hook attachment.
2. Pour in the lukewarm water and crumble in the yeast. Start the machine on the lowest speed and slowly mix for 15 minutes.
3. Add the salt, turn up the speed slightly and mix (knead) for a further 10 minutes.
4. Stop the machine and turn out the bread dough into a large plastic bowl or container. Dust the top of the dough with a little flour and cover the bowl in cling film. Refrigerate overnight. This is called a slow prove.
5. The next day put the dough back in the mixing bowl with the dough hook attached. The dough will have doubled in size. Turn the machine on and, at a low speed, knead for 10 minutes until it becomes silky smooth.
6. Stop the machine and dust a clean work surface with a little flour. Turn out the dough and cut into 3 equal pieces. Knead each piece by hand and shape it into 3 large balls. This process should take about 10 minutes.
7. Dust a large oven tray with flour. Place the bread onto the tray and dust with a little more flour.
8. Wet a clean tea towel with warm water and gently cover the bread. Leave in a warm place to prove for about 2 hours. The ideal temperature would be about 20C.
9. Pre-heat the oven 240C/Fan 220C/475F/Gas 9 and place a small roasting tray in the bottom of the oven with about 1½ inches of boiling water from the kettle. This will create a little steam and make a good crust for the bread.
10. Check the bread has risen and then carefully remove the tea towel. With a sharp knife cut a few decorative incisions on top of the bread, just a cross of about ½ cm deep.
11. Place the bread in the hot oven and bake for about 30 minutes.
12. Remove the loaves from the oven and place to cool on a metal rack, they should be golden in colour and sound hollow when you tap the bottom of each loaf.

# Crispy Garlic Croutons

*Serves 4-6*

**You will need**

1 French baguette, cut into slices

2 tbsp olive oil

1 garlic clove, large

salt

**Method**

1. Cut the baguette into thin slices and lay them on an ovenproof tray.
2. Sprinkle with the olive oil and a little salt and roast in the oven at 180C/Fan 160C/350F/Gas 4 until golden all over and crisp.
3. Peel the garlic clove and cut it in half. With a small sharp knife make several small incisions in both sides of the garlic clove. This will release the oil.
4. Rub each crouton on both sides with the garlic clove. Keep the finished croutons aside until required.

## Wild Garlic

We follow the river into the woods to find wild garlic at the end of April and the beginning of May. There's a wood here that I walk through to get to the old mill where the forest floor is overgrowing with wild garlic. Everywhere you look there's wild garlic – it is like a wild garlic attack! You can smell it, from far away. Even if you are driving with the window down, you will know if there's wild garlic around, especially early in the morning when the oils are released and giving off their odour. The smell is stronger than the taste.

**PIP'S TIP**

## Garlic, White & Pink

This is a tip my dad gave me who uses garlic and onions to cook with almost everything. When I planted our garlic, he told me to remember to knot the stalks together like the French do before they hang them to dry. It is not for decoration; it helps preserve them longer once they have been uprooted.

# Green & Pleasant

*more than a sideshow*

# Pea, Lettuce & Spring Onion Fricassee

### *Serves 4*

**It is June and the peas, lettuces and spring onions are all ready to be picked from the garden. These ingredients make the perfect marriage. Serve this dish as a garnish to a pan-fried duck breast, roast chicken or baked ham.**

**You will need**

1.5kg fresh peas in their pods (you could use 750g of frozen peas, but the taste is not quite the same)

1 bunch of spring onions, about 12 onions

1 lettuce

olive oil for frying

80g butter

1 dstsp of flour

100ml chicken stock, warm

salt and pepper

chopped parsley, chervil, or chives

**Method**

1. Shell the peas and bring them to the boil in a saucepan of salted water. Strain and cover with cold water to refresh and strain again. Trim the lettuce and cut the heart into eight pieces saving a little of the stork to keep it together. Cut and remove the outer skins of the spring onions and remove the green tops. They should be the size of your little finger.
2. In a small bowl add half (40g) of softened butter and mix in 1 dessert spoon of plain flour so it resembles a paste or roux.
3. Place a large frying pan on the stove and heat the oil. Add the peas and fry for two minutes. Add the remaining butter and the lettuce hearts and spring onions. Cook over a high heat. Pour in the chicken stock and when it is boiling stir in the paste/roux a little at a time to thicken. Cook for 2 minutes only. New season peas are very tender and need little cooking time. Season with salt and pepper. Taste. It may need a little lemon juice if too sweet.
4. Pour the fricassee into a bowl and sprinkle with chopped parsley, chervil, or chives.

## Spring Onions & Lettuce

I have been growing spring onions since the start of lockdown. From March they go all the way to September. Now autumn is here, I am planting seeds to get an early spring crop. I absolutely love spring onions in salads and cooked as well.

**PIP'S TIP**

Slugs love lettuces so I sprinkled a circle of ash that I took from the fireplace all around each plant to create a difficult terrain for them to cross. Use crushed eggshells if you can't get any ash.

# Dwarf French Beans with Parsley & Garlic Cream

*Serves 6*

**Pip planted the dwarf beans on 9 July straight after he took out the last of the pea crop. They have grown extremely well.**

**You will need**

- 1.25kg dwarf beans or French beans
- Salt to taste
- 2 egg yolks
- 60ml red wine vinegar
- 90ml double cream
- 80g unsalted butter
- 1 garlic clove, peeled and finely chopped
- 1 small bunch of parsley, picked, washed, dried and chopped
- milled black pepper

**Method**

1. Top and tail the beans. If picked fresh and are young and tender, they will not have any strings.
2. Place a large saucepan on the stove ¾ filled with water. Season with a teaspoon of salt and bring the water to the boil. Add the beans and cover with a lid. Bring the water back to the boil and remove the lid. They will take about 4 minutes to cook.
3. Strain the beans into a colander and cool them down immediately in cold running water. Strain again and set aside in a bowl.
4. Place the egg yolks into a bowl and whisk in the vinegar. Add the cream and whisk until smooth. Season with lots of freshly milled black pepper.
5. Place a large frying pan on the stove to heat. Add the butter to melt and throw in the beans to re-heat. Add the garlic and turn up the heat and fry briefly. Pour in the sauce, cook, and stir for about 1 minute. The cream will thicken, then sprinkle with chopped parsley. Toss them over and pour them out onto a vegetable platter. Serve immediately

It is important not to cook the sauce for too long or the egg yolks will curdle. The sauce is just to coat the beans. Try this with a big fat steak, topped with my herb butter and dare I say some homemade chips cooked in goose fat.

OK as a once a year treat. Red wine with this one!

**PIP'S TIP**

## Dwarf French Beans & Peas

I used a strip of leftover galvanised stock fencing for the plants to grow up. With wooden stakes either side the stalks are supported on all sides and should grow well. We deliberately planted quite densely to get a thicker crop.

# Grilled Courgette Ribbons with Garlic & Olive Oil

*Serves 4*

**This dish was served to Suzi many years ago on a holiday in Sicily and she still loves to replicate it here in Devon. Courgettes seem quite easy to grow and with three rows in the garden we have a plentiful supply.**

**You will need**

8 small courgettes

2 garlic cloves, peeled and crushed to a paste

½ tsp of dried herbs de Provence

3 tbsp of olive oil

1 lemon, juice of

sea salt, lots of

milled black pepper

**Method**

1. Wash and dry the courgettes. Top and tail and lay the courgette flat on a chopping board. With a vegetable peeler or sharp knife starting at one end slice the full length of the courgette. You should get about 4-5 slices per courgette. Repeat this process for the rest.
2 Put the courgette ribbons into a large mixing bowl. Add the chopped garlic and dried herbs. Pour in the lemon juice, olive oil and season with salt and milled black pepper. Carefully mix all together.
3 Lay the courgette ribbons flat on a large roasting tray and grill them under a hot grill to colour.
4 Lift out the courgettes onto a serving plate and serve immediately.

## Courgettes

**PIP'S TIP**

I dug a hole three times the width of the plant pot that the courgettes were started in and twice the depth. I put a couple of inches of fresh chicken manure at the bottom of the hole, filled the rest up with water and waited for it to drain. I put the courgette plants into the hole and covered them with the soil I had dug out. The reason you need that much water is to help establish the roots. Otherwise it takes a lot longer for the plant to adapt from its pot. Make sure you put all the soil that the plant was in into the hole, too, so it does not get a culture shock!

# Simple Buttered Spinach

*Serves 4*

**Spinach has been a huge success in the garden; it turns out it's extremely easy to grow. Having consumed large amounts all summer long we are now extraordinarily strong and healthy. With its high water content there is no need to boil it. Boil it, spoil it.**

**You will need**

400g spinach leaves, washed

1 clove garlic, peeled and crushed

25g butter

Salt and freshly ground black pepper

**Method**

1. Peel the leaves from the centre stalks. This is not necessary if your using baby spinach.
1. Wash the leaves in plenty of cold water to remove any soil. Sometimes it might be necessary to do this twice. Drain in a colander.
2. Place a large saucepan on the stove and add the butter and crushed garlic. When the butter has melted add the spinach and season.
3. Turn up the heat and place a lid on the pan. Cook for no more than 2 minutes. Stir and then cook for a further minute.
4. As soon as the spinach is cooked, pour into a colander, and squeeze out the water with the back of a slotted spoon. Transfer to a serving dish and serve immediately.

## Spinach

**PIP'S TIP**

We all eat spinach in my family and at one stage there was so much of it we were eating it every day. But we had planted so much we could not avoid some of it going to seed. You can tell when that is happening because the leaves start to go pointy. To avoid it happening do not be afraid to chop it right back before it gets too big and high.

# Dig In

*proper dinners*

# A Luxurious Chicken, Mushroom & Bacon Pie

## *Serves 6*

At the end of the shooting season the pheasants that have evaded the gun roam the Devon countryside at will. Inevitably a few succumb to 'roadkill'. Suzi, my wife, hates waste therefore the unfortunate bird will be picked up and brought home to use. Obviously only birds that are not too damaged and relatively fresh are suitable for the pot. At home, this recipe is known as Roadkill Pie. However, for the purposes of looking civilised and politically correct I have used chicken to make this dish, but of course you can use pheasant.

**You will need for poaching the chicken or pheasant**

1 small/medium sized chicken or pheasant

1 onion, peeled and whole

3 garlic cloves, peeled

1 bunch of parsley

1 sprig of tarragon

1 stick of celery, peeled

1 large carrot, peeled

1 glass of dry white wine

1 bay leaf

300ml cold water to cover

**For the pie filling**

1 onion, chopped

4 rashers of streaky bacon cut into lardons

125g mushrooms, peeled and quartered

1 tbsp of olive oil

1 tbsp butter

**For the sauce**

The stock from the poached chicken or pheasant sieved

60g butter

60g plain flour

200ml double cream

a few drops of lemon juice

pinch of salt and pepper

**Method for the bird**

1. To poach the bird, place it in a large pot with all the ingredients and cover with the water. Bring the pot to the boil, skim off any surfacing impurities with a ladle and discard. Turn down the temperature to a gentle simmer and cook for at least 1½ hours.
2. Remove the bird from the cooking liquor and cool.
3. Strain off the liquor through a fine sieve into another smaller pan. Return the liquor to the heat and simmer.
4. Meanwhile strip off the skin from the cooled bird and discard. Now remove all the meat from the carcass. Keep the meat pieces as large as possible and place them into a pie dish.

**For the filling**

1. Fry the bacon, onions, and mushrooms together in a little olive oil and butter, to colour.
2. When golden sprinkle the meat pieces in the pie dish.

**For the sauce**

1. Melt the butter in a saucepan, add the flour and stir it into the butter. Cook until the flour becomes beige in colour and granular (a roux).
2. Add the cooking liquor to the roux, whisking continuously, adding a ladle full at a time. Whisk until all the stock is incorporated.
3. Bring the sauce to the boil and cook it out for 5 minutes. Add the double cream and a little lemon juice. Season with salt and pepper.
4. Strain the sauce and pour over the meat. Leave to cool.

**For the pastry**

1. Pre-heat the oven to 180C/Fan 160C/350F/Gas 4.
2. Stir the flour into a bowl and add the salt.
3. Cut the butter into small pieces and add to the flour. With your fingertips rub together until the mixture resembles fine breadcrumbs. Add the beaten egg and mix to form a dough.
4. Roll the pastry into a ball and cover with cling film and place in the fridge to rest for about 20 minutes.
5. When the pie filling is cool, brush around the edge of the dish with a little egg wash.

**For the pastry**

225g plain flour

165g butter, unsalted

1 pinch salt

1 egg, whole and beaten

1 egg, for egg wash

6. Roll out the pastry to 5-6mm thick. Roll the pastry around your rolling pin and carefully lay it over the pie dish and filling. Crimp the edges of the pastry and any leftover trimmings use to decorate the pie top. Gently brush a little more egg wash over the pastry top.
7. Cook in the pre-heated oven for about 25 – 30 minutes or until golden brown.

Serve with English asparagus and spinach when in season. Peas or purple sprouting broccoli are a great accompaniment. You should not need any potatoes because of the pastry; however, Jersey Royals are delicious!

# Grilled Lemon Sole with Chilli, Chive & Caper Butter

*Serves 3*

With the Devon coast just a mile away, the variety of fish we can catch or buy is truly a gift. Pip is a real fan of this dish especially if he's caught the fish himself. The taste of any grilled fish can be varied by the flavoured butter you serve it with. It also works well for other fish such as mackerel, sea bass, plaice, and the more expensive flat fish such as turbot, brill and Dover sole. See page 128 for Herb Butter recipe.

**You will need**

3 lemon soles about 400g each

20ml olive oil

Salt and ground black pepper

**For the butter**

125g butter, unsalted

1 red chilli, deseeded and finely chopped

bunch chives, chopped

1 dstsp of capers, chopped

1 large garlic clove, chopped

¼ lemon, juice of

salt and pepper to taste

**To prepare the sole**

1. Remove the dark skin from each fish and gut them.
2. Cut off the fins and scale the white skin. Rinse under cold water and then dry on a clean kitchen towel.
3. Place the sole on a flat tray and refrigerate.

**For the butter**

1. Beat the butter until soft and pale.
2. Add the chilli, chives and capers then stir in the garlic. Add the lemon juice and little salt and pepper.
3. Lay out two sheets of greaseproof paper on top of one another and using a spatula place the butter in a line, in the middle of the paper. Fold the paper over and make a sausage shape. Roll the shape and seal the ends like a Christmas cracker then put it in the freezer to set.

**To cook the sole**

1. Pre-heat the oven to 200C/Fan 180C/400F/Gas 6.
2. Oil and season the fish. Place them white skin down onto the tray and cook in the oven for about 6 minutes.

**To serve**

Remove the butter from the freezer. Carefully remove the greaseproof paper and cut it into 6 pieces. Top the sole with the butter and serve. Watercress or samphire makes a good garnish. Serve Jersey Royals, asparagus, and minted peas in season.

## Chives

Chives will grow in almost all soils, but the ideal soil is well dug with well-rotted compost or manure. If you are growing chives indoors, they're best on a sunny south facing window giving the plant between six and eight hours of full sunlight a day. Rotate the chives if they are reaching toward the light to make them grow evenly. And remember to give them a regular haircut!

**PIP'S TIP**

# Summer Vegetable & Lamb Stew

*Serves 4*

**New season lamb and summer vegetables make for a lovely light stew. Our neighbouring farmers both farm rare breed sheep: Fariba and Chris Sutton rear the Black Headed Dorper while Carrie and Trevor Marks have the hardy Herdwick. It always amazes me that this dish can taste so completely different depending on the breed you use. For this stew I have used shoulder of lamb deboned, but you could also use the neck or breast, always cutting off as much fat as possible. The finer cuts of lamb can be costly, but you just as successfully make this using these less expensive cuts.**

**You will need**

1 boned shoulder of lamb cut into large dice or cubes
black pepper and salt.
50g butter
2 tbsp olive oil
1 large onion, chopped
1 large carrot, chopped
1 leek, split and chopped
1 stick of celery, chopped
4 cloves of garlic (smashed)
1 tbsp plain flour
1 bay leaf
1 sprig of rosemary
1 sprig thyme
1 tbsp tomato paste
glass of dry white wine
400ml brown chicken stock
300g baby carrots, whole and peeled
200g potatoes, diced
200g green beans, picked and blanched
150g cherry tomatoes, whole
150g baby courgettes, whole

**Method**

1. Pre-heat the oven to 150C/Fan 130C/300F/Gas 2. Heat a large pan or casserole dish on the stove. Add the oil and just as it starts to smoke add the diced lamb. Add the butter and season with salt and milled black pepper. Colour the meat on all sides.
2. Add the chopped vegetables and cook for a few minutes to soften. Add the flour and stir it into the fat and juices. This will thicken the stew. Cook it to a light brown colour.
3. Now add the tomato puree, garlic, herbs, and the glass of dry white wine.
4. Next stir in the chicken stock, it should just cover the meat. Bring the stew to the boil and skin off all the surfacing impurities, foam and fat with a ladle and discard. Give the stew a good stir to make sure nothing has stuck to the bottom of the pan.
5. Put the lid on the pan or casserole and place it in the oven and cook for about 30 minutes.
6. Now prepare the summer vegetables. Blanch the green beans in boiling salted water for about 3 minutes and then strain. Refresh them in cold water. You can use some ice cubes to help then set aside. Top and tail the baby courgettes and carrots, and top the tomatoes.
7. Remove the stew from the oven and with a slotted spoon transfer lamb to another pan. Strain the sauce through a colander over the meat and discard the cooked vegetables and herbs. Now add the baby carrots and diced potatoes to the stew and cook on top of the stove on a gentle heat for a further 10 minutes.
8. Finally add the blanched green beans, baby courgettes and cherry tomatoes and cook for a further 5 minutes.

I like to sprinkle some chopped parsley over the dish just before serving. You do not need anything with this dish – however, Pip likes a slice of garlic bread as an accompaniment.

**PIP'S TIP**

## Rosemary

A friend gave me a cutting which I put in water and rooted. It was that easy to get it started and it did not cost a penny. We also have an old plant that still flourishes in a pot by the back door.

# A Colourful Vegetable Curry

## *Serves 4*

**This curry uses up most of the vegetables that we have grown in the garden since lockdown. I was amazed just how much stronger the flavour was from a newly pulled garlic bulb, undoubtedly because it is so fresh.**

**You will need**

2 large red onions, finely sliced

30g fresh ginger, grated

4 garlic cloves, crushed

3 large tomatoes, peeled, deseeded, and chopped

1 cinnamon stick

4 cloves

1 tsp cumin seeds roasted in a pan and crushed

1 tsp black peppercorns, crushed

½ tsp chilli powder

½ turmeric powder

½ coriander powder

1 vegetable stock cube, crushed to a powder

1 tbs mild curry paste

50g coconut cream, grated

4/5 kaffir lime leaves

100g carrots, peeled and diced

100g potatoes, peeled and diced

120g cauliflower, cut into florets

100g French beans, cut into 3cm lengths

2 handfuls of baby spinach, washed

5 tbs of vegetable oil

1 dstsp tomato puree

400ml water

salt

**Method**

1. Heat the oil in a thick bottomed pan or casserole dish. Add the cinnamon stick, cloves, roasted cumin seeds, black peppercorns, and sliced onions. Cook on a high heat for about 2 minutes. Add the grated ginger and crushed garlic and continue cooking for a further 2 minutes.
2. Add the chopped tomatoes and cook for 5 minutes and give it a stir.
3. Add the coriander powder, curry paste, vegetable stock cube powder, turmeric, and chilli powder. Stir well and cook for another 5 minutes.
4. Add the water, tomato puree, grated coconut cream and kaffir lime leaves and bring to the boil.
5. Next add the carrots, potatoes and cook for a further 5 minutes. Then add the cauliflower and French beans.
6. Cover with a lid, turn the heat down to a simmer and cook until the vegetables are tender – this will take about 20 minutes.
7. At the last-minute stir in the spinach leaves and check the seasoning. Add salt to taste if required.

I like to leave this curry overnight in the fridge because it is so much better the next day, therefore you could make it the day before you need it.

# Cashew & Saffron Rice

## *Serves 6*

Aromatic and fragrant, here is a rice for any curry.

**You will need**

400g basmati rice
800ml water
4 kaffir lime leaves
6 cardamom pods, crushed
1 cinnamon stick
1 tsp cumin seeds
50g unsalted butter
1 tbsp sunflower oil
100g cashew nuts
1 tsp of saffron threads
3cm fresh ginger, peeled and grated
4 tbsp, live yoghurt
salt and ground black pepper

**Method**

1. Wash the rice in cold water then place it in a bowl covered with 800ml of water. Add the cardamon pod and cinnamon stick, and soak for 15 minutes.
2. Place a frying pan on the stove and heat the oil and half the butter together and fry the cashew nuts until golden in colour. This takes about 5 minutes. When coloured, spoon them out of the pan into a bowl and reserve.
3. Heat the remaining butter in a thick bottomed saucepan over a medium heat and fry the cumin seeds. Immediately add the ginger and seasoning.
4. Drain the rice and whole spices and keep the water for later. Add the rice to the cumin seeds and ginger. Stir for 2 minutes.
5. Add the yoghurt and saffron threads. Pour in the reserved water bring the rice to the boil.
6. Place a lid on the pan, slightly ajar so that the steam can escape and turn down to a simmer. Cook for about 5-6 minutes or until tender.
7. Cover the pan with the lid and reduce the heat to a low simmer for a further 5 minutes. Remove the lid and cover the surface of the rice with the cashew nuts. Now turn off the heat. Replace the lid and leave the rice to gently cook for a further 10 minutes.
8. When cooked stir and fluff up the rice with a fork and transfer it to a serving dish.

# Chicken Rogan John!

*Serves 6*

To make a curry you need good fresh spices, fried first to let loose their wonderful flavours. This is my take on a Rogan Josh and makes excellent use of our fresh tomatoes, garlic, onions and coriander.

**You will need for the chicken**

1 medium size chicken skinned and diced into bite sized pieces or 4 large, skinless chicken breasts diced

4 tbsp of natural yoghurt

1 tsp of garam masala

1 large pinch of pistil saffron

**For the dry ground spices**

1 tsp garam masala,

1 tsp cumin

1 tsp ginger

1 tsp fennel

1 tsp coriander

**For the whole spices**

3 kaffir lime leaves

3 cardamom pods, crushed

1 whole cinnamon stick

1tsp cumin seeds

3 cloves, crushed

**For the sauce**

400g of tinned chopped tomatoes

4 tbsp of clarified butter

3cm pieces of fresh ginger, peeled and grated

2 medium onions, finely chopped

1 fresh red chilli, deseeded and chopped

2 tbsp tomato puree

200g of fresh tomatoes, peeled, deseeded, and chopped

1 large bunch of coriander, picked and chopped

**Method**

Put all the chicken ingredients into a bowl, cover with cling film and marinate, preferably overnight, in the refrigerator.

1. Heat the butter in a large, thick bottom saucepan over a medium heat and gently fry all the whole spices. Add the crushed garlic, ginger, onions, and chilli. Fry for about 5 minutes until the onions are golden in colour.
2. Add the marinated chicken and cover with a lid and cook for 15 minutes. Stir from time to time. Do not let it catch the bottom of the pan.
3. Now add all the ground spices to the chicken and stir in the tomato puree, chopped fresh tomatoes and tinned tomatoes.
4. Stir all the ingredients together and continue cooking for a further 15 minutes until the chicken is cooked through and the sauce thickens.
5. Finally stir in a good handful of chopped coriander leaves. Serve.

I like to cook this curry the day before as its flavour is twice as good the following day. Serve with Cashew and Saffron Rice (see opposite) and Cucumber and Mint Raita (recipe page 120).

# Stuffed Marrow with Parsley & Garlic Crumb

*Serves 4-6*

When you grow and eat your own vegetables, you'll soon change your mind about marrow. I did. Having never bothered with them until Pip raised a bumper crop, I've become something of a convert. I made this dish last night for supper; the marrow weighed in at 1.2 kilos before I prepared it and as you can imagine we only devoured half of it. Sometimes, size really does matter.

**You will need**

1 marrow of 800g

**For the stuffing**

400g lean beef mince, coarsely ground
2 shallots, finely chopped
3 garlic cloves, peeled and finely chopped
1 red pepper, deseeded and chopped
3 tbsp olive oil
2 rashers smoked streaky bacon, cut into lardons
1 red chilli, deseeded and chopped
1 sprig rosemary
1 sprig of thyme
1 tbsp tomato paste
1 tsp sugar
salt and milled pepper
1 glass red wine
1 tin of chopped tomatoes
200ml beef stock
handful of fresh basil
1 tsp Worcestershire sauce
60g butter (to grease the tin foil)

**Method for the stuffing**

1. Heat a saucepan on the stove with the olive oil and add the coarsely ground beef mince. Cook until the meat begins to brown.
2. Add the chopped shallots and garlic and give the mixture a stir.
3. Now add the smoked bacon lardons and cook for about 5 minutes on a high heat.
4. Add the red pepper, chilli and herbs.
5. Stir in the tomato paste and cook for further 5 minutes.
6. Season with sugar, salt and pepper.
7. Pour the large glass of red wine into the pan and bring to the boil. Reduce by half its original volume.
8. Add the chopped tomatoes. Stir, then add the beef stock. Bring to the boil and turn the heat down to a fast simmer.
9. Stir in the fresh basil and add the Worcestershire sauce. Cook for a further 15 minutes and then transfer to a bowl to cool.

**To prepare the marrow**

1. Place the marrow on a board. With a sharp knife top and tail it. Cut it in half from the top to the bottom exposing the seeds (lengthways).
2. Using a dessert spoon scrape out the seeds and discard.
3. Cut two large pieces of tin foil and fold them over in half. With the butter grease the foil and cradle each half of the marrow in the foil, leaving space to stuff the marrow. Place the marrow halves side by side on a roasting pan.
4. Pre-heat the oven 180C/Fan 160C/350F/Gas 4
5. Spoon the filling into the marrow. Place more buttered foil on top and place in the oven. It will take about 1 hour 15 minutes to cook until tender. While the marrow is cooking prepare the crumb.

**PIP'S TIP**

## Thyme

Thyme is a wonderful herb with amazing flavours and Dad uses it all the time. It smells like summer to us. You can use this amazing herb for soups, meat and vegetables. It's a low-growing plant with small leaves and thin, woody stems. When planting, thyme loves the full heat of the sun and well-draining soil. If you're planting in a pot indoors, put it on a sunny windowsill and make sure not to over water.

**For the crumb**

100g cheddar cheese, grated

150g stale bread for breadcrumbs

1 handful parsley, washed and picked

2 garlic cloves, peeled

1 tbsp olive oil

**For the crumb**

1. In a food processor add the parsley, garlic, and stale bread. Blitz for 20 seconds to make a crumb. Add the olive oil and blitz again for a further 10 seconds. Do not overwork the crumb as it will roll into a ball and will not sprinkle. Place the crumbs into a bowl.
2. Add the grated cheese and mix.
3. Check the marrow to see if it is tender and retaining its shape. Now remove the foil from the top and sprinkle on the parsley crumb.
4. Return to the oven and cook for further 15 minutes or until the crumb crisps and turns a golden brown.
5. Remove the marrow from the oven and carefully lift out of the foil cradles and place on a kitchen board or serving plate. Slice into portions and serve.

This dish is a complete meal but if you feel you need something to accompany the marrow, steamed rice works and a mixed salad. I promise you it is so delicious, and I have become a huge marrow fan!

# Hake with Button Mushrooms & Potatoes Boulangère

### *Serves 4*

Hake is a member of the cod family but has a much milder flavour than cod. I use it sometimes for a change. For this recipe you will need 4 thick pieces cut from the middle of the fish. There is some preparation, but the cooking time is relatively quick as the fish is served in individual foil parcels. The flavour of the fish with the mushrooms and potatoes all cooked together is heavenly.

**You will need**

4 x 175g pieces of filleted hake, skinned and pin bones removed

500ml dark chicken stock

500g Maris Piper potatoes or similar

1 onion, peeled and sliced

1 sprig of thyme, leaves pulled from the stalks

1 garlic clove, peeled and finely chopped

salt and milled black pepper

100g butter

1 tbsp olive oil

200g button mushrooms, finely sliced

1 tbsp parsley, chopped

truffle oil to serve

4 pieces of greaseproof paper

4 pieces of foil

(each measuring 45 x 60cm for the parcels)

**Method**

1. Pre-heat the oven to 200C/Fan 180C/400F/Gas 6.
2. Bring the chicken stock to the boil in a large pan. Peel and slice the potatoes into 5mm thick slices. Add them to the stock with the sliced onion and thyme leaves. Bring the liquid to the boil and cook for about 5 minutes or until the potatoes are tender but still hold their shape. Carefully strain them into a colander over a bowl.
3. Season the fish. Heat half the butter and the olive oil in a frying pan and sear the fish on both sides for two minutes to colour but not cook. Remove the fish from the pan and set aside on a tray.
4. Heat the remaining butter in the pan, add the mushrooms, garlic, and seasoning. Cook until golden brown then sprinkle with the chopped parsley. With a spatula remove the mushrooms to a tray and set aside to cool.
5. To make the parcels, lay one piece of greaseproof paper on the work surface and place a sheet of foil on top with a long edge facing you. Arrange ¼ of the potato and onion slices on the foil slightly off centre, overlapping to form a bed. Place a fillet of hake on top of the potatoes and scatter the mushrooms over the top.
6. Bring the far corners up to meet the near corners, starting from the left corner and working all the way around to the other side, and fold over 3cm of the paper and foil at a time to seal. The parcel will resemble a pasty. Repeat this process for the remaining hake fillets.
7. Place the parcels on a baking tray and cook in the pre-heated oven for 12 minutes.

**To serve**

Open the parcels at the table and hand around some truffle oil to drizzle over the top. I like to eat this dish with podded broad beans and smoked bacon lardons.

# Potato Gnocchi with Butternut Squash Puree, Charred Baby Leeks & Sage

## *Serves 6*

**Pip and I are extremely pleased with our first attempt at growing potatoes – we have a plentiful crop and, to go with it, countless potato recipes. This is a very satisfying dish to make.**

**You will need for the gnocchi**

500g dry (no butter) warm potato puree (mash) = 6 medium size potatoes

4 egg yolks

150g plain flour

80g Parmesan cheese, grated

50g shallots, chopped

10g parsley, chopped

2 garlic cloves, peeled and finely chopped

salt and milled white pepper

**You will need for the butternut puree**

1 medium butternut squash or small pumpkin

2 tbsp olive oil

3 garlic cloves, peeled and crushed

150g butter, diced

sprig of thyme

double cream (a splash)

**You will also need**

handful of sage leaves

12 baby leeks, trimmed and blanched

1tbsp olive oil

40g Parmesan cheese, finely grated

**Method for the gnocchi**

1. Bake 6 medium size potatoes in a pre-heated oven at 180C/Fan 160C/ 350F/Gas 4 for about 40 minutes. The skins should be dark, crisp and the flesh inside soft. Just press a potato with your index finger and thumb to feel if they are ready. Do not burn yourself!
2. When the potatoes are cooked, cut them in two lengthways and with a dessert spoon scrape out the potato flesh into a bowl.
3. Heat a frying pan with a little butter and cook the shallots, no colour, just to soften, and add the chopped garlic. Remove the pan from the stove and put the shallots and garlic on a plate to cool.
4. When cooled firstly add the shallots to the potato puree then the grated Parmesan cheese, parsley and egg yolks.
5. Sieve the plain flour and add to the mixture and season with a little salt and milled white pepper.
6. Very gently mix all the ingredients together.
7. Dust a work surface with a little flour. Cut the gnocchi mixture into two pieces and with a rolling pin roll the mixture out to form two sausage shapes the width of a wooden spoon handle.
8. Cut the gnocchi into 1cm pieces. Pick up the pieces one by one and roll the gnocchi over the back of a fork to make a mark.
9. Place them in the refrigerator on a tray lined with greaseproof paper until needed.

**To cook the gnocchi**

1. Place a large pan half filled with water on the stove and bring it to the boil. Drop half the gnocchi into the pan, they will fall to the bottom and rise to the top as they cook. Scoop them out and with a slotted spoon immediately place them into ice-cold water to cool. Do not leave them in the water. As soon as they are cold scoop them out onto a clean dry tea towel.
2. Keep in the fridge until needed.
3. Repeat this process for the second batch.

**Method for the butternut squash**

1. Cut the butternut squash into 8 pieces. Remove and take out the seeds.
2. Place the butternut squash in a roasting tray with its skin on and a little olive oil with the garlic and thyme. Cover with foil and bake in a pre-heated oven at 180C/Fan 160C/350F/Gas 4 for about 1 hour. When cooked remove the foil. Scrape out the flesh from the skin. Put the flesh and cooked garlic in a liquidiser and blitz to a puree.
3. Pour the puree into a pan. Over a medium heat add the butter piece by piece and stir it into the puree. Add a splash of double cream. Season with salt and pepper and keep warm. I like to stir in a little truffle oil, but the preference is yours.

**To serve**

1. Sprinkle the grated Parmesan cheese into 6 ring moulds placed on a non-stick oven mat and bake in a pre-heated oven at 180C/Fan 160C/350F/Gas 4 for 3 minutes or until golden brown and crisp. Remove the tray and the ring moulds and lift off the Parmesan crisps with a palette knife.
2. Re-heat the gnocchi in a little foaming butter with the fresh sage leaves until nut brown.
3. At the same time warm the puree in a small pan and pour a little onto a large plate or bowl and place the gnocchi on top.
4. Place the blanched baby leeks on an oven tray with a little olive oil under a hot grill and cook to colour.
5. Place the baby leeks across the top of the gnocchi.
6. Finally top the dish with the Parmesan crisps.

**PIP'S TIP**

## Leeks

I start my seedlings off in the greenhouse spaced into a big pot to grow into tall and established plants before I turn them out into the garden. I leave them about a week outside in the pot to acclimatise before planting. It is also less of a shock for the plant as you move it to the earth to grow tall and thick.

# Roast Loin of Pork with a Walnut Crumb & Rhubarb

*Serves 6*

**Pork and apples are a well-loved combination. So is pork with gooseberries or plums. But perhaps best of all is pork with rhubarb. With this dish I remove the outer skin, but do not panic, crackling lovers, it is roasted on a separate tray. The walnut crumb gives a wonderful deep and earthy flavour. A neighbouring farmer has a walnut tree in his drive which gives a plentiful yield. His Jack Russell terrier sits underneath to guard the nuts from opportunistic squirrels.**

**You will need**

1.75kg pork loin, skin removed (keep the skin for crackling)

1 lemon, zest of preferably unwaxed

2 garlic cloves, peeled and sliced

1 tbsp parsley, chopped

salt

20ml vegetable oil

100g walnuts

100g fresh bread

50g soft butter

400g rhubarb, young rhubarb cut into batons 5cm long

200g caster sugar

2 tbsp water

1 tbsp elderflower cordial (optional)

300ml white wine

300ml chicken stock

1 medium size cabbage, quartered, core removed and chopped

**Method**

1. Pre-heat the oven 190C/Fan 170C/375F/Gas 5.
2. Peel the zest of the lemon. Turn it over and with a sharp knife carefully slice off any white pith. Put the zest in a small pan and cover it with cold water. Bring it to the boil and then drain. Repeat this process another time, cooking for about a minute each time. This will soften the lemon and remove all the bitterness. Finally refresh the zest in cold water and when cold drain, then dry it on clean kitchen paper or tea towel. Set aside.
3. With the point of a small knife, score the pork fat on top of the loin by making several incisions in the fat. Poke a little lemon zest into each incision. Poke in the garlic slices and push in the chopped parsley.
4. Sear the joint in a frying pan with a little oil, fat side down first. Place it in the oven in a roasting tray and cook for about 30 minutes at the same time on a separate oven tray place the reserved pork skin, sprinkle with salt and cook until crisp and golden then remove and keep the crackling warm.
5. After half an hour remove the pork and carefully tip off any fat. Pour in the wine and return the pork to the oven for about 40 minutes.
6. Meanwhile, with a food processor blitz the walnuts and bread together to make a crumb. Add the butter and blitz again to form a soft paste.
7. Take the pork out of the oven and carefully tip out any cooking juices into another small saucepan and set aside. Press the walnut crumb onto the fatty side of the pork so that it is evenly coated. Turn down the oven to 140C/Fan 120C/275F/Gas 1.
8. Return the pork to the oven and continue cooking until it is golden brown.
9. To cook the rhubarb, place it in an ovenproof dish. Sprinkle it with caster sugar the water and elderflower cordial. Place it into the oven to cook until tender this should take about 10 minutes.
10. Cook the chopped cabbage in boiling salted water until tender. Drain and keep to one side.
11. Add the chicken stock to the pork cooking juices and bring it to a fast boil. Reduce by half to concentrate the flavours of this sauce.

**To serve**

Re-heat the cabbage in a little of the sauce. Season with salt and pepper and spoon it down the centre of the plate.

Place the pork on a chopping board and slice two slices per person and lay it on top of the cabbage. Arrange some batons of rhubarb on the side or on top and pour a little sauce around. Place a piece of warm crackling on top of the pork. Delicious.

**PIP'S TIP**

### Rhubarb

Dig a deep hole and dig in some well-rotted manure before planting the rhubarb. Rhubarb likes space and sunshine so decide the spot for your plant because it will not want to move.

Rhubarb seems to have a mind of its own and is very hardy. Dad loves using rhubarb so it was a must to plant. It remains dormant in the cold winter months then comes to life in the spring and summer. It is easy to grow so we just leave it alone until Dad needs it for one of his recipes.

# Tempura of Sole with Parsley, Spinach & Watercress Sauce

*Serves 2*

**Tempura batter is ethereal, light and crisp. I designed this recipe for sole but large prawns would work just as well. I can't resist tempura-battered courgette flowers or elderflowers when in bloom dipped, fried and dusted with icing sugar.**

**You will need**

4 large fillets of sole, Dover or lemon, skinned and cut into fingers half a centimetre wide and 4cm long. You will need 100g of fish per person

**For the batter**

100g plain flour

50g cornflour

½ tsp baking powder

250ml cold sparkling water

2-3 ice cubes

**Method**

1. Sieve the flour and cornflour into a bowl. Add the baking powder.
2. Whisk in the ice-cold sparkling water and add the ice cubes.
3. Season the sole and dip the fish into the batter.
4. Fry in hot sunflower or vegetable oil until golden.
5. Drain the fish on several layers of kitchen paper and serve immediately. Serve a wedge of lemon and the Parsley, Spinach and Watercress Sauce (recipe on page 126

# Dexter Beef Pie with Spitfire Ale

## *Serves 6*

For the small cocktail onions in this dish I boil them in water for two or three minutes, strain off the water and once cool enough to touch I just pod and peel the skins off. You can serve this pie with seasonal fresh vegetables from the garden. You will need a large pudding or pie dish.

**You will need for the pastry**

225g plain flour

pinch salt

75g butter, diced

75g lard, diced

1 egg beaten, for the egg wash

1 tbsp of cold or iced water

**For the pie filling**

200g baby silver skinned or pickling onions

200g button mushrooms

100ml sunflower oil

900g diced Dexter Beef (chuck steak)

1 onion, chopped

1 carrot, chopped

1 dstsp tomato paste

1 tsp Worcestershire sauce

2 sprigs of thyme

1 dstsp of English mustard

120ml Spitfire or similar ale of your choice (drink the other half)

120ml beef stock

salt and milled black pepper

**Method**

1. Sieve the flour into a bowl and add the salt. Add the butter and lard and with a knife cut the fat into the flour. Avoid using your fingers as this will melt the fat and ruin the consistency of the pastry. Add some cold or iced water a little at a time and mix the pastry to form a dough.
2. Roll it into a ball, wrap it in cling film and chill in the fridge.

**For the filling**

1. Place a large frying pan on the stove with a little sunflower oil and fry the mushrooms and baby (blanched) onions to colour. When brown put them into a bowl to cool.
2. In the same frying pan heat the remaining oil and add the beef. Fry to colour and add the finely chopped onion and carrot.
3. Add the tomato paste, stir, and cook it out for about 2 minutes. Add the thyme and Worcestershire sauce.
4. Stir in the mustard and pour in the Spitfire ale. Bring the pan to the boil and add the beef stock. Season with salt and milled black pepper. Turn down the pie filling to a gentle simmer and cook it for about 1½ hours or until the beef is tender.
5. Remove the pan from the stove and pour the contents into a bowl to cool.
6. Take the pastry from the fridge and allow it to come to room temperature.
7. On a floured work surface cut the pastry in half. Roll out one half of the pastry and fold the outside into the centre, repeat for the other half. Fold the pastry over and return it to the fridge. Repeat this process (turn) for both halves of pastry.
8. Remove the pastry from the fridge. Roll one piece out to about 5mm thick and line the base of the pie dish. Pour in the cooled beef mixture. Roll out the second piece of pastry to the same thickness. Egg wash around the inside of the dish and lay down the pastry top over the pie.
9. Pre-heat the oven to 200C/Fan 180C/400F/Gas 6.
10. Using a rolling pin, roll gently over the top of the pie to seal the pastry edges. With your forefinger and thumb, crimp around the edge of the pie.
11. Carefully cut away any excess pastry and use it to decorate the top. Brush the top of the pie with the remaining egg wash and cook it in the oven for 20 minutes until golden brown.

This is a great traditional pie and relatively cheap to make. Drink a cold bottle of Spitfire to accompany this delicious meal. You will not be disappointed.

# Grilled Lobster with Garlic, Herb & Chilli Butter

## *Serves 2*

This is an absolute treat – serve on an incredibly special occasion.

**You will need**

1 lobster 700g split in two, large claws cracked, and entrail/gut line removed

½ lemon, juice of

2 tbsp olive oil

salt and milled black pepper

50g of Herb Butter (see recipe on page 128)

**Method**

1. Place the lobster onto a small metal roasting tray flesh side up. Sprinkle with olive oil and season with salt and black pepper. Squeeze the lemon juice over the lobster.
2. Place under a hot grill for about 5 minutes. Remove the lobster and top each half with the garlic, herb and chilli butter and continue to grill for a further 5 minutes.
3. Remove from the grill and serve immediately.

I love this dish served with Parmesan and Anchovy Salad (right) and a glass of champagne.

# Parmesan & Anchovy Salad

## *Serves 4*

**You will need**

2 little gem lettuces, cut in half or 1 large romaine lettuce

2 tbsp olive oil

1 tbsp white wine vinegar

1 tsp lemon juice

1 pinch of salt

milled black pepper

1 pinch sugar

½ garlic clove, chopped

2 tbsp double cream

1 tbsp mayonnaise

1 tbsp Parmesan, finely grated

3 filets of Spanish anchovies, finely chopped

**Method**

1. In a mixing bowl add the olive oil and whisk in the white wine vinegar. Add the seasoning and the pinch of sugar.
2. Stir in the garlic, double cream, and mayonnaise. Add the grated Parmesan and chopped anchovy and stir gently.
3. Separate the lettuce hearts and add to the dressing in the bowl. Mix the lettuce until it is thoroughly coated in the dressing.
4. Place the coated lettuce on a plate and serve.

# Grilled Mackerel with Capers, Lemon & Parsley

*Serves 4*

In late spring and summer Pip and I head to the beach at Torcross to fish for mackerel on the high tide. On a good day we might land up to 120 of them. We keep our quota and take the rest to our local pub in Slapton in exchange for supper. Mackerel is a beautiful, oily fish rich in omega 3 fatty acids. I pair this dish with potato salad and some dressed lettuce from the garden.

**You will need**

4 large mackerel, filleted and boned

2 tbsp of olive oil

salt and milled black pepper

1 lemon, peeled and segmented

1 clove of garlic, crushed and chopped

1 tbsp of capers, drained

60g butter

50ml chicken stock or stock cube

1 tbsp chopped parsley

**Method**

1. Prepare the mackerel and place it onto a shallow ovenproof tray skin side up. Pour the olive oil over the fillets and season with a little salt and lots of milled black pepper.
2. Top and tail the lemon and carefully following the contours of the fruit slice off the skin, rind, and pith. Follow the first cut and remove all the skin from the fruit. With a small knife cut in between the segments and repeat the process. Put the segments into a small bowl.
3. Peel, crush and chop the garlic clove. Reserve and set aside.
4. Pick, wash and dry the parsley and finely chop.
5. Heat a pan on the stove. Add the butter and as it melts and starts to foam add the lemon, capers, and garlic.
6. Pour in the chicken stock and bring the sauce to the boil and add the chopped parsley.
7. Pre-heat the grill and when it is hot, place the mackerel under and grill for two minutes to colour the skins. Remove the mackerel from the grill. Pour the sauce over the fish and serve immediately.

I place the hot tray full of mackerel on top of a chopping board and let everyone help themselves. The intense smell is so delicious.

# Smoked Haddock with Spinach & Chive Butter Sauce

*Serves 4*

**I use undyed smoked haddock, not the bright yellow one which is dyed in turmeric and goodness knows what else. We're on a roll now with our spinach. On top of the first abundant crop, a second lot will be ready in September. You can't beat homegrown fresh young spinach leaves. Chives from the herb garden really elevate this dish.**

**You will need for the butter sauce**

150g unsalted butter

1 shallot, peeled and finely chopped

1 garlic clove, peeled and finely chopped

1 sprig of thyme

½ bay leaf

1 sprig of fresh tarragon

1 tbsp white wine vinegar

60ml white wine

3 tbsp double cream

juice of ½ lemon

salt and milled black pepper

1 tbsp of chopped chives

**For the haddock**

750g smoked haddock, cut into 4

250ml milk

freshly milled black pepper

50g butter

**For the spinach**

400g spinach picked washed and dried

25g butter

salt and milled black pepper

nutmeg, a little grated

**Method for the sauce**

1. In a saucepan melt 25g of butter and add the chopped shallots and garlic, thyme, bay leaf and tarragon. Fry the ingredients together but with no colour.
2. Add the vinegar, bring to the boil, reduce the liquid until it is almost evaporated then add the wine and boil again until syrupy. Pour in the cream and boil again.
3. Dice the remaining butter and while the sauce is boiling whisk in the butter, piece by piece, until it has completely dissolved.
4. Add the lemon juice and seasoning. Heat the sauce but do not boil it at this stage, whisking all the time. Strain it through a fine sieve into another pan.
5. Stir in the chopped chives and keep warm.

**For the haddock**

1. Place a large frying pan on the stove. Pour in the milk, add the butter, and freshly ground black pepper. Bring the milk to a gentle simmer. Add the haddock, cover with greaseproof paper, and poach for about 8 minutes.
2. Heat a saucepan on the stove and add the spinach, seasoning, and a little grated nutmeg. Add the butter and gently stir. It should cook in 2 minutes then remove from the heat. A large amount of water will come out of the spinach so drain this off by pouring it into a sieve over the sink and force out the water by pressing with the back of a spoon.
3. Divide the spinach in four and spoon it onto the centre of four plates.
4. With a fish slice lift out the haddock and place it on top of the spinach.
5. Spoon the warm chive butter sauce over the fish and serve.

# Eight Confit Duck Legs

*Serves 8 (one each)*

**You will need**

8 duck legs

600g duck fat or pork fat

100g sea salt

50g sugar

3 bay leaves

2 sprigs of thyme

4 juniper berries crushed

1½ dstsp black peppercorns, crushed

3 garlic cloves, crushed

**Method**

1. Place the duck legs in a deep roasting tray and sprinkle with all the ingredients. Place in a refrigerator overnight.
2. The next day wash off all the salt mixture under plenty of cold running water and thoroughly dry.
3. Place the duck legs back into the roasting tray and cover them with the duck fat. Cook in the oven for about 2 hours at 160C/Fan 140C/325F/Gas 3 until golden brown.

Serve with potato dauphinoise, green beans.

# Braised Beef in Red Wine

*Serves 8*

**Even in remote Devon, the growing trend for food delivery boxes has not passed us by. There are some super beef producers on our doorstep and we look forward to our 'beef box', a selection of prime cuts delivered to our home. I particularly like Dexter cattle, a little Irish breed half the size of a Hereford with beautifully tender, flavoursome meat and good marbling. Huge fan.**

**You will need**

2kg beef, used topside, chuck or rump cut into eight pieces or 2cm cubes

250g smoked bacon cut into 5mm strips

50ml ground nut oil

1 litre beef stock or a stock cube

salt and pepper

2 tbsp chopped parsley to garnish

**For the marinade**

1 bottle of red wine, you can use Rioja, Cabernet Sauvignon, or a Malbec

2 garlic cloves, peeled and crushed

1 bay leaf

2 sprigs of thyme

2 strips of orange rind

1 onion, chopped

1 leek, chopped

1 carrot, chopped

2 sticks of celery, chopped

**Method**

You will need a large casserole dish or heavy bottomed pan with a lid.

Place all the ingredients in a bowl and marinate overnight. Once marinated strain the beef reserving the marinade and other ingredients.

1. Heat a large pan on the stove with a little oil. When the oil starts to smoke place in the beef and sear it to colour. Transfer to a large casserole dish.
2. In the same pan, fry and colour the vegetables reserved from the marinade and when brown pour them over the beef.
3. Cover the beef with the bacon strips, herbs, and garlic.
4. Pre-heat the oven to 180C/Fan 160C/350F/Gas 4.
5. Pour the strained marinade into a large frying pan and boil it to deglaze and reduce by half its volume, then pour it over the beef in the casserole. Pour in the beef stock and bring to the boil. Cover with a lid and cook in the oven for about 1½ hours or until tender.
6. When the beef is cooked carefully lift it out and put it in a serving dish to rest.
7. Meanwhile bring the sauce to the boil and thicken. It should coat the back of a spoon. Strain the sauce through a fine sieve and then pour over the beef.

I like to garnish this dish with glazed baby onions or shallots, button mushrooms and a few bacon lardons. Sprinkle with chopped parsley and garlic croutons.

**PIP'S TIP**

## Parsley, Curly & Flat leaf.

There are two main types of parsley. Curly leaf looks good as a garnish but is a lot milder in taste than flat leaf, which is stronger, more versatile, and easier to prepare. Parsley can be harvested throughout the year. Grow it in a cold frame or indoors during winter. For the best flavour, pick parsley during the day when the plant's oil is strongest.

# Cheese, Onion & Smoked Bacon Flan made with Cheddar & Poppy Seed Pastry

*Serves 6-8*

**Makes 1 x 28cm flan tin. This pastry works for savoury flans and tarts. It is thin and crisp and makes for a slightly more interesting texture.**

**You will need for the pastry**

180g plain flour plus a little extra for dusting

pinch of salt

110g unsalted butter plus a little extra for greasing

1 tbsp cold water

1 egg

1 tsp of poppy seeds

25g cheddar cheese, grated

**For the filling**

1 medium onion, finely sliced

30g butter

125g smoked streaky bacon

2 eggs

150ml milk

150ml crème fraiche or whipping cream

salt and milled black pepper

a little grated nutmeg

1 tbsp chopped parsley

100g strong cheddar cheese or gruyere cheese

**Method**

1. Sieve the flour and salt into a mixing bowl.
2. Cut the butter into cubes and add it to the flour. Rub the butter into the flour between your thumb and fingers until the mixture resembles fine breadcrumbs.
3. In a jug or small bowl beat the egg together with the cold water and poppy seeds. Pour into the flour mixture and add the grated cheese.
4. Carefully bring the ingredients together to form a ball. Do not overwork the pastry.
5. Lightly knead the pastry on a floured work surface, then wrap it in cling film and refrigerate for at least 30 minutes before use.

**For the filling**

1. To line the flan tin, cut the chilled pastry in half and roll one piece out on a clean work surface dusted with flour. The circle of pastry needs to be 2-3 mm thick and slightly larger than the flan ring.
2. Pick up the pastry by rolling it onto the rolling pin, then hold it over the flan dish and unroll the pastry so that it lays over the top of the dish. Pick the edge of the pastry up with one hand and use the other hand to ease the pastry into the corners of the dish, working all the way round.
3. Press your thumb right around the rim of the dish to neaten the edge of the flan case, then cut away the excess pastry. Prick the pastry base all over with a fork and put the flan case in the fridge to chill for 30 minutes.
4. Pre-heat the oven at 200C/Fan 180C/400F/Gas 6.
5. Cut a circle of greaseproof paper enough to cover the base and sides of the flan. Place it in the pastry case and pour in the baking beans or use raw rice to keep the paper weighed down.
6. Bake the flan case for 15 minutes then remove from the oven and lift out the beans and paper. Be careful the beans will be hot. Return the flan case to the oven and continue cooking for another 5 minutes or until the pastry is golden brown and crisp. Set aside and turn the oven down to 160C/Fan 140C/325F/Gas 3.
7. In a frying pan over a medium heat add the sliced onions and butter and cook gently, stirring occasionally until the onion is soft.
8. Grill the bacon for a few minutes on each side, then allow it to cool before cutting it into strips (lardons).
9. Whisk the egg, milk and cream together and add some salt, pepper and nutmeg to taste. Stir in the chopped parsley.
10. Put the softened onion in the base of the flan case. Top with grated cheese and bacon, then pour in the egg mixture.
11. Carefully place the flan into the oven and bake for 20-25 minutes or until the eggs are set and the surface of the flan is a golden brown.

As an alternative try substituting the onions for leeks, smoked salmon cut into strips instead of bacon and goats' cheese instead of cheddar. Mix some chives into the egg mixture instead of the parsley.

# Oxtail with Mustard & Herb Dumplings

## *Serves 4*

**Oxtail is popular nowadays no doubt for its rich flavour and value for money. Cold, flaked and mixed with grated Parmesan in a homemade ravioli with fresh sage butter, it is heaven. Oxtail soup garnished with boiled basmati rice or in a mulligatawny is delightful. This recipe is simple and cheap.**

**You will need**

2 oxtails cut into sections about 2½ cm thick

2 tbsp of plain flour for dusting the ox tails

salt and lots of milled black pepper

40g dripping or lard

2 large carrots, chopped

1 stick of celery, peeled and chopped

2 onions, peeled and chopped

2 garlic cloves

1 tbsp flour

1 tbsp tomato puree

25ml dry sherry

half bottle red wine

750ml beef stock

1 tsp of Worcestershire sauce

1 bay leaf

2 sprigs of thyme

**For the dumplings**

250g plain flour

125g shredded suet

salt

½ tsp of dry mustard powder

1 tsp baking powder

½ tsp fresh thyme, picked and washed

water to bind

**Method for the oxtail**

1. Dust the oxtail pieces in seasoned flour.
2. Melt the lard or dripping in a large pan and fry the oxtails on both sides until brown in colour. This takes about 10 minutes. Remove the oxtails and place them into a large casserole dish.
3. In the same pan add the vegetables and garlic and fry to colour. Sprinkle in the flour and add the tomato puree and stir well.
4. Pour in the sherry and boil to reduce.
5. Pour in the red wine and bring it to the boil.
6. Add the beef stock and the bay leaf, thyme, Worcestershire sauce and season with salt and pepper.
7. Pre-heat the oven to 140C/Fan 120C/275F/Gas 1.
8. Skim off any surfacing impurities and discard. Pour the contents over the oxtails. On the stove bring the casserole to the boil, place on the lid and cook in the oven for about one and a half hours or until the meat is tender and beginning to fall off the bone. Meanwhile prepare the dumplings.

**For the dumplings**

1. Sieve the flour into a bowl. Add the mustard powder and baking powder. Add the salt.
2. Rub in the suet and add the thyme.
3. Bring the dumplings together with a little cold water, about 2 tablespoons to make a dough.
4. Shape the dough into small balls the size of a large golf ball or larger if you like a bigger dumpling.
5. 30 minutes before serving remove the lid of the casserole and drop the dumplings into the cooking liquor and leave off the lid. They will cook and expand in the oven making a crunchy top and soft below.

Serve with celeriac puree, glazed turnips, buttered kale, or mashed swede.

# Spaghetti with Smoked Bacon, Parsley Crumb & Garlic

### *Serves 4-6*

**Sometimes even I cannot be bothered to cook at supper time, so this is a favourite quick no bother dish. It is moreish and uses up stale bread from the bread bin.**

**You will need**

1 x 500g packet spaghetti or fresh pasta

200g smoked streaky bacon

1 large onion, finely chopped

4 cloves of garlic, finely chopped

3 tbsp of olive oil

100g butter, unsalted

200g white breadcrumbs (coarse)

1 handful of parsley, picked, washed, dried, and chopped

Parmesan cheese peeled with a vegetable peeler, as much as you want

milled black pepper

**Method**

1. Place a large frying pan on the stove to heat. Add 2 of the tablespoons of olive oil.
2. Cut the rashers of bacon into lardons about 2cm wide and add them to the pan. Cook gently to extract all the fat and flavour from the bacon, this takes about 10 minutes.
3. Add the chopped onions to the bacon, stir and cook gently without colour to soften.
4. Stir in the garlic and immediately add the butter.
5. Sprinkle in the breadcrumbs and gently cook. They will absorb all the flavour in the pan. Cook to colour, a golden brown. Keep moving and stirring the pan they must not burn.
6. Put a large saucepan on the stove filled ¾ of the way up with water. Season with salt and add the remaining olive oil and bring the water to the boil. All at once add the spaghetti. Stir the pan and the spaghetti will slowly slip into the water. Boil for about 10 minutes for dry pasta to cook and 3 minutes for fresh pasta.
7. When cooked strain the pasta into a colander over the sink and shake off any excess water.
8. When the breadcrumbs are golden, sprinkle and stir in the chopped parsley.
9. Put a portion of spaghetti into a serving bowl and put the breadcrumb mixture over the top.

Season the dish with lots of black pepper. I love Parmesan cheese, so I sprinkle a good amount over the breadcrumbs with a swirl of good quality olive oil. You can use your preferred cheese. A mature cheddar works just as well.

**PIP'S TIP**

## French Beans

When the beans start to appear and are ready to pick, it is easy to let many go to waste. Be sure to check the thickest leaves at the bottom of the plant where they are growing densely but out of sight. They are usually the best ones.

# Battered John Dory with a Spiced Mayonnaise

*Serves 6*

This dish is great any time of the year. It works with cod and haddock. You will need 6 fillets about 110g-120g per person. The seriously good sauce has a mayonnaise base.

**You will need for the sauce**

200g mayonnaise

50ml double cream

¼ lemon, juice of

1 tbs capers, chopped and squeezed

1 tbs gherkins, chopped

1 tsp mild curry powder

1 shallot, finely chopped

1 tbs parsley, chopped

1 tbs chervil or dill, chopped

1 small red chilli, deseeded and chopped

black pepper and salt to taste

**For the John Dory**

Ask your fishmonger to fillet 3 medium sized fish. You will need 2 fillets per person about 100g for each serving. That makes 650g in total (skinned weight). If not available use cod or haddock

**For the batter**

125g plain flour

60g cornflour

½ tsp baking powder#

½ tsp bicarbonate of soda

1 tsp mild curry powder

225ml of larger (cold)

salt and milled black pepper

Some seasoned flour for dusting

**Method**

1. In a large bowl pour in the double cream and stir in the mayonnaise. Squeeze a little lemon juice and stir.
2. Squeeze the vinegar or brine from the capers and finely chop them. Stir into the sauce. Finely chop the gherkins.
3. Add all the remaining ingredients and mix well. Season with milled black pepper and salt. Keep it in a glass bowl in the refrigerator before serving.

**For the John Dory**

Fry the fish in vegetable or sunflower oil. You will need 1 litre.

**For the batter**

Mix all the ingredients together in a bowl. Do not add the lager until the last minute, just before frying. Make sure when adding the lager, you mix with a whisk vigorously and continuously to avoid any lumps.

**The frying**

1. Pour the oil into 2 large saucepans and heat it to 160C/Fan 140C/325F/Gas 3. Make sure the oil level is no more than a third of the way up the pan.
2. If you do not have a thermometer test the oil by dropping in a little batter, it should rise to the top of the oil straight away and bubble.
3. Pre-heat your oven 140C/Fan 120C/275F/Gas 1.
4. Dust the fillets with seasoned flour and drop then one by one into the batter. Fry to colour on both sides to a golden brown. With a slotted spoon remove the fillets to a tray. You must do this process in stages to avoid losing too much heat in the oil. Store the fillets in the oven until all the fish is fried.

Serve this dish with the spiced mayonnaise and thin chips. Drink a glass of lager or chilled Muscadet. I like a tomato and red onion salad to accompany this dish.

# Poached Brill with Lemon & Chive Butter Sauce

*Serves 4-6*

**OK, so the idea behind this book is for affordable but incredible recipes. If I could think of a cheaper substitute for brill or turbot I would but there isn't one so this is for those special gatherings that only come up once or twice a year. Poach the fish whole or cut it into portions.**

**You will need**

1.5kg of fish (brill or turbot). You can ask your fishmonger to prepare the fish for you

**For the poaching liquor**

1 carrot, peeled and sliced
1 stick of celery, peeled and sliced
1 bulb of fennel, thinly sliced
1 large onion, sliced into rings
1 leak, trimmed and sliced
3 cloves of garlic, peeled and crushed
100ml white wine
1 tsp crushed white peppercorns
1 tsp coriander seeds
2 sprigs of thyme
½ a lemon, sliced
1 tsp of salt
1 litre of water

**For the sauce**

2 shallots, peeled and finely chopped
2 tbsp of white wine vinegar
150ml of dry white wine
1 clove of garlic
1 sprig of thyme
50ml double cream
200g unsalted butter
¼ lemon, juice of
2 tbsp chives, chopped
salt and pepper

**Method to prepare the fish**

1. Using a pair kitchen scissors, cut off all the fins and trim the tail.
2. Cut out the gill and discard. Check to see if the fish has been gutted properly, if not remove any guts and discard.
3. If you want to poach the fish whole place it in a large deep roasting tray and prepare the cooking liquor.
4. To portion the fish, trim of the head by making a semicircular cut behind the head. Avoid cutting into the flesh.
5. Starting at the tail, cut down the middle of the fish and with a clever or heavy knife cut the fish against the bone and divide it in two.
6. Cut each half into three equal pieces of the same weight.

**For the poaching liquor**

1. Peel and slice the vegetables and place them in a large saucepan with the remaining ingredients. Top with the water and bring it to the boil.
2. Turn down the heat to a simmer and cook for 10 minutes for all the ingredients to infuse.
3. Strain the liquor through a sieve into another pain. Place the fish in the pan and gently simmer for about 7-8 minutes, depending on how thick the fish is.
4. Remove the fish from the pan and very carefully peel off the skin. At this stage you can carefully remove the flesh from the bones. Place it on a serving dish covered with cling film to keep warm.

(This poaching liquor recipe also works with poached salmon or lobster).

**For the sauce**

1. In a small pan melt a little butter and add the shallots. Cook to soften, no colour.
2. Add the vinegar, garlic and thyme; turn up the heat to the boil to reduce the liquid to a thick syrup.
3. Add the white wine and boil. Reduce the wine by about ½ until it becomes syrupy again.
4. Pour in the cream and bring it back to the boil.
5. Dice the remaining butter and, whisking all the time, add it piece by piece to the pan to melt.
6. Continue whisking until it is fully absorbed into the sauce. Strain the butter sauce through a sieve into another pan. Add the chives and lemon juice. Season to taste.

**To serve**

I like to serve this dish with a little steamed cabbage, new potatoes, green beans, and buttered spinach. All the spring veg!

# Make a Beeline

*for puds*

# Old Fashioned Egg Custard Flan

*Serves 6*

We like to travel to France as least once a year and, stopping on the autoroute de soleil at L'Arche, a French chain of cafeterias, to buy a slice each of tarte au flan à la Parisienne. Back home, I make as close a version as I can to remind us of happy days. I use guinea fowl eggs when I can find their nests to make this flan. The eggs are smaller than a chicken's, but the yolks are incredibly rich and work just perfectly.

**You will need**

24cm deep flan ring (make sure it is at least 2½ inches deep)

A baking sheet lined with greaseproof paper

250g ready-made pure butter puff pastry

500ml whole milk

120g sugar

1 vanilla pod, split and seeds scarped out but saved

3 eggs, beaten

60g custard power or cornflour

60g butter

1 egg, beaten for egg wash

**Method**

1. Pre-heat the oven at 190C/Fan 170C/375F/Gas 5.
1. Roll out the puff pastry to about ½ cm thickness larger than the flan ring. Place the flan ring on the baking sheet lined with greaseproof paper. Line the ring and press the pastry up around the top to make a border of about ½ cm above the ring. With a fork prick the pastry base to stop it rising when cooking.
2. With a rolling pin, roll over the top of the flan ring and remove the overhanging pastry.
3. With your thumb and forefinger raise the pastry border up above the edge and place it in the freezer to set.
4. Heat the milk with half the sugar and the vanilla seeds in a pan. In a bowl whisk the eggs and the remaining sugar until pale in colour and thickened.
5. Whisk half the hot milk into the egg and return the mixture to the remaining milk in the pan.
6. Whisk in the custard powder or cornflour and cook, whisking continuously until smooth. DO NOT BOIL. Remove from the heat and whisk in the butter.
7. Using a spatula transfer the custard filling to the chilled flan. Brush the top of the filling with egg wash and bake for about 30 minutes. The top will go very dark but do not be put off. This is called blistering and is the desired effect.

# Summer Strawberry Tart with Pistachio Crumb

### *Serves 6-8*

In a sunny corner of the vegetable garden we planted 8 strawberry plants grown from seed in the greenhouse in spring. With such a good spring and early summer, they ripened quickly. The riper the strawberry the sweeter the taste. This recipe uses our ripe strawberries and the combination of sweetness and acidity is perfect with the rich pastry cream.

**You will need for the sweet pastry**

150g unsalted butter

60g icing sugar

1 egg

250g plain flour

28cm fluted tart tin

**For the pastry cream**

500ml whole milk

1 vanilla pod

50g plain flour

50g cornflour or custard powder

6 egg yolks

110g caster sugar

**Method for the sweet pastry**

1. Mix the butter and icing sugar together and beat it in a bowl by hand until it starts to become light in colour.
2. Add the egg and beat to a smooth paste.
3. Sieve the flour and mix until it starts to come away from the sides of the bowl.
4. As soon as the pastry comes together mould it into a ball. Wrap it in cling film and place it into the refrigerator for about one hour.
5. Remove from the fridge and roll it out onto a floured surface. Keep the pastry as cold as possible. Do not over handle it.
6. Line the tart ring and return the tart to the fridge to set for about 30 minutes.
7. Remove the tart and lay it down on a baking sheet. Line the top with greaseproof paper and fill it with baking beans or raw rice.
8. Pre-heat the oven to 200C/Fan 180C/400F/Gas 6.
9. Bake in the oven for 15 minutes. Remove the tart from the oven and remove the paper and beans. Then return the tart to the oven and cook until it becomes golden in colour. This will take about a further 10 minutes.
10. When cooked take it out of the oven and set aside to cool.

**For the pastry cream**

1. Bring the milk to the boil in a saucepan with the vanilla pod (split into two lengthways).
2. In a small bowl mix the plain and cornflour together.
3. In a separate bowl whisk the egg yolks and sugar together until they become pale and thick. Then mix in the flour.
4. Gently pour approximately 1/3 of the boiling milk over the egg yolks and sugar. Whisk together until smooth. Add this back into the milk in the saucepan.
5. Bring the pastry cream back to the boil whisking vigorously all the time.
6. When it has boiled and thickened, using a spatula pour it into a bowl. Cover with cling film and when cold place it in the refrigerator. You can make this the day before as it keeps for about 3 days.

**For the strawberry filling**

350g medium sized strawberries (hulled and cut in half)

2 tbsp strawberry jam

2 tbsp water

50g pistachio nuts, green and peeled

60ml water

80g caster sugar

**For the strawberry filling**

1. With a spatula stir the pastry cream and place it in a piping bag.
2. Pipe the pastry cream into the tart base.
3. Slice the strawberries in half and arrange them in a circle on top of that tart, working from the outside in. Leave a whole strawberry for the centre.
4. In a small pan on the stove over a medium heat gently melt the strawberry jam with the water. Once the jam has melted pour the glaze into a sieve and push it through into a small bowl to remove any of the whole fruit or seeds.
5. With a pastry brush carefully brush the strawberries with the glaze.
6. To make the pistachio crumb put the sugar into a small pan with the water. Cook on the stove boiling the syrup until it thickens and starts to colour, a light caramel colour. As soon as it starts to colour add the pistachio nuts and quickly remove the pan from the heat and pour the pistachio nuts out onto a tray. They will cool and harden very quickly.
7. When cold break up the pistachio brittle with a rolling pin and pound it to a breadcrumb consistency.
8. Alternatively, you can put the pistachio brittle into a food processor for the same effect.
9. Finally, before serving sprinkle the strawberry tart with the pistachio crumb.

This is a delightful treat and can be served for a special occasion. It is that good!

PIP'S TIP

## Strawberries

In late May I placed straw in rows along and under the fruit trusses to keep the weeds back and stop the fruit from lying on the ground and spoiling. I recommend using barley straw as it is soft, and it is advisable to net your strawberries to stop the birds from eating them.

# Rice Pudding with a Summer Fruit Compote

*Serves 6*

**Devon has some of the best grazing in the British Isles. A dairy farm right on our doorstep means a continuous supply of fresh milk. This recipe is one of life's simple pleasures, rich, creamy, and the definition of ambrosia.**

**You will need**

200g pudding rice or arborio

1 litre of whole milk

2 vanilla pods, split lengthways and seeds scraped out

100ml double cream

2 egg yolks

120g undyed caster sugar

1 pinch salt

**For the compote**

50g strawberries, washed and hulled

50g raspberries, washed and hulled

50g blackcurrants, washed

1 vanilla pod, split

100g undyed caster sugar

**Method**

1. Place all the fruit into a pan with the split vanilla pod and sugar.
2. Continuously stirring bring the fruit mixture to the boil until all the sugar has dissolved.
3. Transfer the fruit compote into a bowl to cool and reserve for later.
4. Next in a pan bring 500ml water to the boil. Add the rice and cook it for about 2 minutes to release the starch from the grains then drain it through a sieve.
5. In a separate pan, bring the milk, vanilla seeds and sugar to the boil.
6. Add the rice and cook stirring all the time do not stop. Add the pinch of salt and stir the rice until all the milk has been absorbed. This takes about 20 minutes, but it is worth it.
7. When cooked pour the rice into a bowl. Stir in the double cream and the two egg yolks. The heat from the rice will cook the egg yolks.

**To serve**

You can serve the rice pudding hot or cold with the fruit compote. I prefer it cold. I measure the amount of cooked rice and fold half the amount of whipped double cream into the cold rice pudding. Yum!

# Simple Luscious Lemon Tart

## *Serves 6*

There are lots of lemon tart recipes doing the rounds, this one is quick and easy but add wild strawberries and it's off the charts. Luckily, we have them growing all over the garden. They are much smaller than the cultivated variety but much sweeter. They are a special little fruit for just a fleeting time in the year.

**You will need for the sweet pastry**

28cm fluted tart tin

150g unsalted butter

60g icing sugar

1 egg

250g plain flour

100g of white chocolate, melted

**For the lemon cream**

150ml freshly squeezed lemon juice

(about 3 large lemons)

3 eggs, beaten

120g caster sugar

1½ leaves of gelatine about 3g

75g butter, unsalted and soft

icing sugar for dusting

**Method for the pastry**

1. Mix the butter and icing sugar together and beat it in a bowl by hand until it starts to become light in colour.
2. Add the egg and beat to a smooth paste.
3. Sieve the flour and mix until it starts to come away from the sides of the bowl.
4. As soon as the pastry comes together mould it into a ball. Wrap it in cling film and place it into the refrigerator for about one hour.
5. Remove from the fridge and roll it out onto a floured surface. Keep the pastry as cold as possible. Do not over handle it.
6. Line the tart tin and return the tart to the fridge to set for about 30 minutes.
7. Remove the tart and lay it down on a baking sheet. Line the top with greaseproof paper and fill it with baking beans or raw rice.
8. Pre-heat the oven to 200C/Fan 180C/400F/Gas 6.
9. Bake in the oven for 15 minutes. Remove the tart from the oven and remove the paper and beans. Then return the tart to the oven and cook until it becomes golden in colour. This will take about a further 10 minutes.
10. When cooked take it out of the oven and set aside to cool.
11. Melt the white chocolate in a small bowl over a saucepan of hot water. When the tart base is cold. Brush the warm chocolate over the base and sides of the tart. Refrigerate to set for 10 minutes.

**Method for the lemon cream**

1. Put the lemon juice, eggs and sugar into bowl, over a saucepan of hot water. This is called a bain-marie. Whisk the ingredients together until it thickens. The lemon mixture needs to reach a temperature of 60C.

1. Meanwhile soak the gelatine leaves in a bowl of cold water to soften.
2. Remove the bain-marie from the heat and take the bowl off the saucepan. Squeeze off the water from the gelatine and stir into the lemon mixture until dissolved. Mix the butter with an electric stick blender into the mixture then set aside to cool.
3. Pour the lemon cream into the tart base. Fill it to the top and smooth it over with a palette knife.
4. Refrigerate to set. Dust with icing sugar just before serving

Serve with fresh raspberries or strawberries.

# Sweet Cherry & Amaretto Tart

*Serves 6*

The season for British cherries is from early summer with a later crop arriving in September usually from Scotland. We have a small cherry tree here in the garden but to date it has not produced enough fruit to make a single tart. These were made with supermarket-bought cherries and very good they were, too. I make this tart with a lovely sweet short crust pastry because it has a wonderful crunchy texture.

**You will need for the pastry**

26cm tart tin

150g unsalted butter

60g icing sugar

1 egg, large

250g plain flour

**For the filling**

2 eggs

1 egg yolk

10g plain flour

40g caster sugar

125ml milk

125ml double cream

300g fresh pitted cherries

1 tbsp Amaretto

icing sugar for dusting

**Method for the pastry**

1. In a bowl, beat the butter and icing sugar together until it becomes pale in colour and fluffy.
2. Add the egg and beat to a smooth paste.
3. Sieve the flour into the paste and mix it until it comes away from the sides of the bowl. As soon as it comes together mould it into a ball and wrap it in cling film and place in the refrigerator to rest for about an hour.
4. Dust a clean work surface with a little flour, then take out the pastry from the refrigerator and roll it out. Line a tart tin so that the pastry stands 1cm above the top of the tin. Cut a circle of greaseproof paper 4 inches wider than the tart tin. Carefully place it on the base of the tart and fill it with raw rice or baking beans. Return the tart base to the refrigerator to cool for at least 1 hour.
5. Pre-heat the oven to 180C/Fan 160/350F/Gas 4 and blind bake the pastry for about 15-20 minutes.

**For the filling**

1. In a bowl, whisk the eggs and egg yolk together. Add the sugar and continue whisking.
2. Add the flour, milk, and cream and mix to form a batter. Now add the Amaretto.
3. Carefully place the pitted cherries into the base of the tart and pour the batter mix over the fruit.
4. Place in the oven and cook for 35 minutes at 180C/Fan 160C/350F/Gas 4 or until set.
5. Remove from the oven and allow to cool. When cold remove the tart from the tin and dust with a little icing sugar.

I like to serve this dish with a little whipped cream.

# Dinner Party Dark Chocolate Delice with Salted Caramel Sauce

## *Serves 14*

I love chocolate. If I could grow a cacao tree in the garden I would. This dessert is one of my favourites and is great for a special occasion. With a soft sponge base topped with a rich chocolate mousse it is simply delightful. I love to serve it with red fruits and a puddle of cream or with a salted caramel sauce.

**You will need for the sponge**

28cm cake ring

2 egg yolks

2 tbsp of cold water

40g caster sugar

2 egg whites, plus 15g caster sugar

50g plain flour

50g 70% dark chocolate, melted (to brush the sponge base)

icing sugar for dusting

**For the delice**

6 egg yolks

80g caster sugar

250ml milk

250ml double cream

350g 70% dark chocolate, melted

150ml double cream, lightly whipped

chocolate powder for dusting

**Method for the sponge**

1. With an electric mixer, beat the egg yolks, water and caster sugar together until it reaches 4 times its original volume.
2. In another bowl whisk the egg whites to soft peaks and gradually add the sugar.
3. Mix 1/3 of the beaten egg whites into the egg yolk mixture. Then gently fold in the remainder. Sieve in the flour and using a spatula fold the mixture from the bottom of the bowl to the top gently turning it over. Do not over mix or you will knock the air out of the sponge.
4. Use non-stick baking parchment or a silicone mat placed on a baking sheet. If using greaseproof paper brush the surface with a thin layer of melted butter dusted with a little flour, then pour the sponge mixture as evenly as possible and with a palette knife spread evening over the tray.
5. Pre-heat the oven to 200C/Fan 180C/400F/Gas 6. Bake the sponge for 6-8 minutes or until golden brown.
6. Remove the sponge from the oven. Take a 30cm metal cake ring without a bottom and press it down into the sponge to make the cake base.
7. Melt the chocolate in a bowl over a pan of hot water, stirring continuously and with a pastry brush, cover the top of the sponge. This will add a crunch to the base. Set aside to cool.

**Method for the delice**

1. With an electric mixer, whisk the egg yolks and sugar together until pale in a bowl.
2. In a large saucepan bring the milk and cream to the boil and pour it into the egg mixture. Pour all the ingredients back into the pan and cook until it begins to thicken stirring continuously with a whisk. DO NOT BOIL or you will have scrambled egg and not a custard.
3. Pour the custard mixture over the melted chocolate and whisk until smooth. Allow to cool.
4. Lightly whisk the double cream and fold it into the chocolate mixture. This is the delice.
5. Pour the delice over the sponge base in the cake ring and refrigerate to set.
6. Remove the delice from the fridge and with the point of a warm knife carefully cut round the cake ring to release it. Dust the top with a little chocolate powder.

**For the caramel sauce**

125g caster sugar

15ml water

75ml double cream

75g unsalted butter, diced

pinch of salt, large

**For the caramel sauce**

1. In a saucepan cook the sugar and water together until caramel in colour. Take the pan off the heat and whisk in the cream.
2. Return the pan to a gentle heat and piece by piece add the butter stirring continuously until fully incorporated.
3. Add the large pinch of salt and stir. Pour the sauce into a jug to cool.

**To serve**

With a hot knife cut a portion of the delice and pour a little sauce around the plate.

# Apricot & Almond Tart

*Serves 6*

Our garden faces south-west and the autumn winds sometimes wreak havoc with the apples in the old orchard. The delicate apricot would hate it here hence we do not have one. However, we have a friend who grows this fabulous fruit against a warm sun-drenched wall in her garden and she is more than happy to share her limited crop with us.

**You will need for the pastry**

26cm pastry ring

60g unsalted butter

45g icing sugar

15g ground almonds

1 egg, beaten

pinch of salt

125g plain flour

**For the almond cream**

45g unsalted butter, softened

45g caster sugar

1 egg, beaten

45g ground almonds

10ml double cream

**For the apricots**

500g of ripe apricots, cut in half and stones removed

1 tbsp apricot jam

1 tbsp water

**Method for the pastry**

1. Cream the butter and sugar together in a bowl until smooth. Add the ground almonds and the beaten egg.
2. Add a pinch of salt and sieve the flour. Mix to form a ball and wrap the pastry in cling film and place it in the refrigerator.

**For the almond cream**

1. Whisk the butter in a bowl until pale, add the sugar but do not over beat it. Whisk in the egg and stir in the ground almonds.
2. Pour in the cream and stir. Refrigerate to cool.

**For the apricots**

1. Pre-heat the oven 180C/Fan 160C/350F/Gas 4.
2. Line a baking tray with baking parchment and place the pastry ring on top.
3. Dust a little flour onto your work surface and roll out the pastry. Wrap it around the rolling pin and line the tart ring. Make sure the pastry sits up about ½ cm above the lip of the ring.
4. Carefully pour the almond cream into the tart base and smooth it level with the back of a tablespoon.
5. Arrange the apricot halves on top of the almond cream and bake in the oven for 25 minutes or until golden.
6. Remove the tart and allow it to cool.
7. Meanwhile warm the apricot jam and a little water in a small saucepan to make the glaze.
8. Carefully brush the glaze over the cold apricot tart and serve.

Try this dish with almond ice cream or a splash of double cream.

**PIP'S TIP**

## Greenhouse

I purchased my greenhouse very cheaply during lockdown. I was advised by a well-respected gardener to plant marigolds in the greenhouse to attract ladybirds, which eat aphids and their eggs. It seemed to work.

# Lime Posset, Strawberry Jelly, and Candied Lime Zest

*Serves 6*

**A quick, light, and delicious dessert. I use our super ripe strawberries for this dish.**

**You will need**

2 leaves of gelatine, soaked to soften

500ml double cream

125g caster sugar

juice of 4-5 limes zest removed

**For the strawberry jelly**

250g strawberries, hulled

65ml grenadine syrup

250g caster sugar

250ml water

1 vanilla pod, split and seeds scraped out

50ml vodka

2 leaves of gelatine, soaked to soften

**Method for the posset**

1. Soak the leaves of gelatine in a bowl of cold water for 5 minutes or until soft.
2. Put the cream into a saucepan, bring it to the boil, turn it down to a simmer and cook for further 3 to 4 minutes
3. Add the squeezed and strained lime juice and cook for a further 4 minutes. Remove the pan from the heat.
4. Squeeze the excess water from the gelatine and stir it into the cream until completely dissolved.
5. Now pour the posset through a fine sieve into a jug, then pour it into individual serving glasses or bowls.
6. Put the possets into the refrigerator overnight to set.

**For the strawberry jelly**

1. Place the sugar, vanilla and water into a pan and heat gently until the sugar has dissolved. Stir the liquid and do not let it catch.
2. Take out half the syrup and pour it into another pan and set aside for the lime zest. Heat the remaining syrup, take the pan off the heat, and add the grenadine and vodka. Stir in the soaked gelatine to dissolve.
3. Finally slice the strawberries into a bowl and then pour the syrup over them. Set aside to cool. When cool spoon the jelly over the posset and return to the refrigerator to set.

**For the candied lime zest**

1. Using a small knife, remove all the pith from the lime zest. Blanch the zest in boiling water for three minutes, refresh in ice water. Strain off the water and repeat this process, twice more or until the zest is tender.
2. Put the pan with the remaining syrup on the stove to boil. Cut the lime zest into thin strips and place them into the boiling syrup, boil and reduce the liquid by a third.
3. With a fork remove the zest from the syrup and place on a tray to cool and dry. The lime zest should be translucent and soft.

To assemble the possets, remove from the fridge, top them with a little candied zest and just for decoration fresh strawberry flowers if you have them.

# Chocolate Orange Cake

## *Serves 6-8*

If you like Jaffa Cakes you will love this recipe. This is one of Pip's favourites and, understandably, no one else gets a look-in.

**You will need**

20-22cm cake tin with a false bottom

175g caster sugar

175g unsalted butter

4 eggs, beaten

2 tbsp bitter chocolate powder

50g ground almonds

175g self-raising flour

1 tbs hot water

1 tbsp marmalade

**For the filling**

zest and juice 1 large unwaxed orange

juice of ½ a lemon

50g unsalted butter

2 eggs

1 egg yolk

60g icing sugar

1 tbsp cornflour

80ml double cream

**For the chocolate topping**

175g chocolate (no less than 60% cocoa solids)

150ml double cream

25g butter

**Method for the cake**

1. Grease the cake tin and dust it with flour. Shake off the excess.
2. With an electric mixer beat the butter and sugar together until it becomes pale and fluffy. Pour in the beaten egg and add the chocolate powder and ground almonds.
3. Sieve the flour and add it to the mixture on a slow speed until fully incorporated.
4. Add the tablespoon of hot water
5. Pre-heat the oven to 180C/160F/350F/Gas 4. With the aid of a spatula pour the cake mixture into the tin. Cook for about 35 minutes. The cake should feel springy to the touch when cooked. Allow to cool.
6. When the cake is cold, carefully cut it in two through the middle with a sharp knife. Spread the marmalade over both halves and put to one side.

**For the filling**

1. Place a saucepan half filled with water on the stove. Bring it to a high simmer or rolling boil.
2. Grate the orange zest into a bowl. Squeeze out the juice of the orange and lemon over the zest. No pips.
3. Add the eggs and egg yolk, sugar, and butter. Whisk over the hot water until the mixture thickens. Add the cornflour and continue whisking. The whole process takes about ten minutes to make the curd.
4. Remove the orange curd from the stove and leave it to cool.
5. Whip the cream and gradually stir it into the curd. Refrigerate to set.
6. When set, spread the orange curd filling onto the bottom of the cake. Lift the top and gently press it down to re-form the cake.

**For the chocolate topping**

1. Gently melt the chocolate in a bowl over a pan of simmering water. When melted stir in the butter. Allow to cool a little.
2. Whip the cream. Do not over whip: lightly whipped ribbons. Slowly stir the cream into the chocolate.
3. With a palette knife cover the cake with the chocolate mixture. Refrigerate to set.

# Classic Egg Custard Tart

## *Serves 8*

We are incredibly lucky to have a rainbow flock of chickens, large fowl, and bantams of varying types. But it's the guinea fowl whose eggs are so wonderfully rich and make this dish the most amazing yellow colour. This dish can be served on its own or with a strawberry compote. It is also delicious served with stewed greengage plums. You may use the Strawberry Tart with Pistachio Crumb pastry recipe (p88). It is a sweet, short crust pastry and ideal for this tart. Bake it blind filled with baking beans or rice placed on greaseproof paper.

**You will need**

For the tart base you will need a quantity of sweet, short crust pastry and one egg beaten to seal the tart.

**For the egg custard**

28cm tart tin

400ml single cream

200ml whole milk

1 vanilla pod and seeds

1 pinch of freshly grated nutmeg or ground

60g caster sugar

3 whole eggs

2 egg yolks

1 egg for the egg wash

**Method**

1. Pre-heat the oven 180C/Fan 160C/350F/Gas 4. Roll out the pastry and line the tart tin.
2. Blind bake the tart with baking beans or rice over a circle of greaseproof paper. Cook for about 20 minutes.
3. Remove the tart case from the oven and remove the beans carefully. Brush the tart with beaten egg and return the tart to the oven and bake for a further 5 minutes. The egg wash will seal the pastry. Remove the tart to cool.
4. Pour the cream and milk into a saucepan. Add the split vanilla pod and seeds and grate in some nutmeg. Bring the mixture to a gentle boil.
5. In a mixing bowl whisk the sugar, eggs and egg yolks. Pour in the milk and cream whisking all the time. Remove the vanilla pod and wash it under a cold running tap. Dry it on some clean kitchen paper. (This can then be used to flavour your sugar. Keep it in a Kilner jar covered with caster sugar for your baking. Do not waste any part of the vanilla pod – they are awfully expensive.)
6. With a small ladle or spoon skim off all the surfacing foam and air bubbles from the custard and discard.
7. Carefully pour the custard into the tart base. Turn down the oven to 140C/Fan 120C/275F/Gas 1 and place the tart in the oven to bake. It will take 25-30 minutes to set with a wobble.
8. Remove the tart and leave it to cool.

It is best to eat the tart on the same day. If you put it in the fridge it will get a soggy bottom, and nobody likes a soggy bottom!

# Homemade Vanilla Custard

*Makes 600ml*

I love custard hot or cold. Occasionally Pip ventures up the road to the dairy farm to fill a bottle with some delicious raw milk, full fat and perfect for making custard. Raw milk has not been pasteurised and can contain some bacteria; however, I am still alive and kicking with no adverse effects and of course you can use pasteurised whole milk instead. I like to use our own free-range eggs as their yolks are an intense yellow colour. Slice some ripe bananas into a bowl, pour in some cold custard and a drizzle of Rose Hip Syrup.

**You will need**

500ml fresh whole milk

8 egg yolks

100g caster sugar

1 vanilla pod split

**Method**

1. Pour the milk into a saucepan. Split the vanilla pod and scrape out the seeds. Put it into the milk, stir it with a small whisk and bring to the boil.
2. Separate the eggs, place the yolks in a large bowl and whisk them together with the sugar until they become pale in colour.
3. Take the milk off the stove and little by little add the milk to the egg and sugar mixture stirring all the time.
4. Transfer the mixture to a clean pan and place the pan over a low heat, it will start to thicken and cook the egg yolks. It should coat the back of a spoon. Do not boil as this will cause the custard to curdle.
5. Remove from the heat and serve hot or cold.

You can subtly change the flavour of the custard by infusing lemon or orange zest into the milk or add 10g of instant coffee powder for a coffee custard.

# Baked Apples stuffed with Dried Fruits & Somerset Apple Brandy

*Serves 4-6*

**The old Bramley apple trees in our garden are still soldiering on. Year after year they keep on delivering to us their fruit for dishes both savoury and sweet. Baked apples are a quintessential autumn dessert even if we do eat them all year round. Bring on the lashings of homemade custard, crème fraiche or ice cream.**

**You will need**

4 large bramley apples, cored not peeled

50g sweet, dried cherries

50g sultanas

50g golden raisins

50g walnuts, chopped

2 Medjool dates chopped

100g sugar

pinch of ground cinnamon

large dash of Somerset apple brandy or Calvados

125g butter

**Method**

1. Place all the dried fruit and walnuts in a bowl. Add the sugar and apple brandy. Add a pinch of ground cinnamon and cover with cling film and allow the fruit to absorb the alcohol.
2. Core the apples and put them into a roasting tray or an ovenproof dish with a lip.
3. Pre-heat the oven at 160C/Fan 140C/325F/Gas 3.
4. Fill the apples with the mixture and pour a little water into the dish. This will help the apples to cook evenly.
5. Cut the butter into slices and place it on top of the apples. Cover with tin foil and place in the oven for 35-40 minutes.
6. After 20 minutes remove the foil and with a spoon baste the apples with all the juices and butter in the tray. Return them to the oven to continue cooking. Do not let them get too soft or they will lose their shape.
7. Take them to the table from the oven. They smell simply great and serve with homemade custard.

**PIP'S TIP**

## Bramley Apples

Somewhere back in our family history, on my mother's side, her ancestor Mary Ann Brailsford planted a pip that became the first Bramley Apple tree some 200 years ago. Maybe that's why I'm called Pip! We have some lovely old, gnarled apple trees in our little orchard which still produce some fine apples.

# Fig & Almond Tart

## *Serves 4-6*

This is one of my favourite tarts. I love figs but if they're not available I use apricots or plums. You will need black dessert figs as opposed to green ones which are great preserved or in chutneys.

**You will need for the pastry**

28cm tart tin or dish

85g unsalted butter (softened)

70g icing sugar

pinch of salt

100g plain flour

1 tsp mixed spice

1 egg yolk

**For the filling**

400g black desert figs

70g ground almonds

70g light brown cane sugar (soft)

70g butter diced and softened

1 tbs Amaretto (optional)

1 egg

1 tbs flaked almonds

**For the glaze**

50g clear honey

1 orange, zest and juice of

**Method**

1. Dice the butter and place it in a bowl. Add the sugar and salt and beat it together until creamy and pale in colour.
2. Add the flour and mixed spice and gently work the dough together. Add the egg yolk to bind.
3. Dust a work surface with a little more flour and roll out the pastry. Lift the pastry into the tart tin or dish and cut away any excess from the top. Place the tart in the refrigerator to set. This takes about half an hour.
4. Pre-heat the oven to 180C/Fan 160C/350F/Gas 4.
5. Line the tart base with greaseproof paper and bake blind with baking beans or rice for 15 minutes. No colour but cooked. Allow to cool.

**For the filling**

1. In a bowl add the butter and sugar together and mix well. Stir in the ground almonds and if you wish add the Amaretto.
2. Beat in the egg.
3. With a plastic spatula fill the tart base and smooth level.
4. Wash and dry the figs. Cut each fig into 6 vertically.
5. Arrange the figs skin side down starting on the outer rim of the tin working in towards the centre overlapping slightly.
6. Sprinkle with flaked almonds.
7. Place the tart back in the oven for a further 15 minutes until golden.

**For the glaze**

Warm the honey in a small pan, add the juice and zest of 1 orange and mix. Brush the warm tart with the glaze and serve.

This dish is lovely with almond or pistachio ice cream or gelato.

# Apple, Plum & Hazelnut Crumble with a dash of Damson Gin

*Serves 6*

**We have three lovely old Victoria plum trees and some very gnarled Bramley apple trees in the orchard. Apples and plums together in a pie or crumble are incredible. A dash of damson gin makes this crumble just a little bit special. Serve a dollop of clotted cream or clotted cream ice cream with it, which being in Devon comes with the territory.**

**You will need for the filling**

2 large Bramley apples, peeled and cored
6 large ripe plums, stones removed
75g golden caster sugar
40g unsalted butter
1 vanilla pod, split seeds scraped out
good slug of damson gin (optional) – see p125

**For the crumble**

100g butter
100g caster sugar
150g plain flour
50g toasted, peeled, and chopped hazelnuts

**Method for the filling**

1. Pre-heat the oven 180C/Fan 160C/350F/ Gas 3
2. Peel, core and dice the apples into quarters and each quarter into three. Cut the plums in half and place in a bowl.
3. Place a large frying pan on the stove to heat.
4. Sprinkle the sugar over the fruit. Split the vanilla pod and scrape out the seeds. Place the seeds and pod into pan.
5. Add the butter, as it starts to melt add the fruit. Cook until the sugar starts to caramelise then add the slug of damson gin.
6. Pour the fruit mixture into a large ovenproof dish and set aside.

**Method for the crumble**

1. Cut the butter into cubes and place it into a bowl. Add the flour and carefully rub together with your fingertips until it resembles large breadcrumbs. Do not over work.
2. Sprinkle in the sugar and gently mix.
3. Top the fruit with the crumble mix and bake it in the oven for 20-25 minutes or until golden.
4. After 20-25 minutes, remove the crumble, sprinkle the toasted, chopped hazelnuts on top and return the crumble to the oven it should take a further 5 minutes. Serve hot with cream, custard or ice cream.

### Plums

**PIP'S TIP**

Check them regularly and pick before the wasps get to them. I pick them in the early morning to avoid the wasps. Unfortunately, most plums get a fungus growing which looks like mould. If you pick the younger ripe fruit you may avoid this.

# Steamed Honey & Orange Sponge Pudding with Homemade Custard

## *Serves 4*

**For a comforting sweet, I love an old-fashioned sponge pudding. A friend of ours gave Pip his first beehive to initiate him into the world beekeeping and harvesting honey. Having our own honey is a pure, unadulterated luxury.**

**You will need**

2 pint or 1.2 litre pudding basin

50g butter (for greasing the basin)

3 tbsp of pure honey (for the bottom of the basin)

175g softened butter

175g golden caster sugar

1 orange, zest finely grated

4 medium eggs

1 tbsp pure honey (in the mixture)

175g self-raising flour

1 heaped tsp baking powder

**Method**

1. Grease the pudding basin with the 50g of butter and carefully add the 3 tablespoons of honey into the bottom of the basin.
2. In a mixing bowl with a whisk attachment whisk the 175g of butter and sugar together until it becomes pale in colour, this takes about 3 minutes.
3. Add the orange zest and one by one beat in the eggs to a smooth paste and add the tablespoon of honey.
4. Sieve the flour and baking powder together and with a spatula mix all at once, into the butter and eggs.
5. Carefully spoon the sponge mixture into the basin and gently level off the top with a palette knife.
6. Wrap the pudding with a layer of greaseproof paper and two layers of tin foil. Tie the rim of the basin with string.
7. Place a large pan, half filled, with water onto the stove and bring it to the boil. Put the basin into the pan and turn down the heat to a simmer.
8. The pudding will take up to 2 hours to cook so keep checking on the water level in the saucepan. Top up with boiling water from the kettle as necessary.
9. To serve: with a cloth carefully remove the basin from the saucepan. Cut the string and remove the layers of paper and foil. With a small knife loosen the pudding from around the edge. Place a large serving plate over the top of the pudding and quickly turn it over. The weight of the sponge will release it from the basin, and it should drop onto the plate.

Serve with homemade custard. Recipe page 103.

FRANCE

# Put a Label on It

*preserves and more*

# Blackberry Jelly

Blackberries are plentiful in the hedgerows of Devon from about August onwards. Pip and I make blackberry jelly most years and sell the jars at the top of the drive in our honesty box. It is a very versatile product. We use it to accompany roast lamb, stirred into game sauces, used as a glaze for sweet tarts or simply spread on hot buttered toast for breakfast. A homemade blackberry syrup topped off with champagne makes the perfect Bramble Royale.

**You will need**

1.5kg freshly picked blackberries, washed

550g jam sugar

**Method**

1. Cook the blackberries gently simmering in a large pan for about 30 minutes.
2. When the blackberries are cooked pour them into a large muslin cloth doubled over or fine tea towel placed over a thick bottomed pan to drain. Leave to drain overnight if you can. You should yield about 700ml of juice. Pre-heat the oven to 140C/Fan 120C/275F/Gas 1.
3. Add the sugar to the blackberry juice and bring to the boil in the pan for about 30 minutes skimming off any surfacing impurities and discard. Stir occasionally.
4. Wash the jam jars and rinse thoroughly. On an oven tray place them upside down. Turn the pre-heated oven off and put the jam jars in to dry.
5. Once the jelly is cooked, leave it to cool slightly then pour it into the dry jars. Let it cool, fit the lids and put them in a cupboard or fridge.

**PIP'S TIP**

## Blackberries

I absolutely love blackberries and can admit to eating almost my own body weight in them, as I walk up the lane picking them straight from the hedgerow on the way to my part-time job. I discovered that the taste is more intense from the small ones.

# Crab Apple Jelly

*Makes 3 jars*

**In spring, the old crab apple tree right in front of the house appears to bend under the weight of its blossom. It usually yields pounds and pounds of apples and it would be foolish not to make jelly. The jelly is pink as a jewel and has a sweet and sour flavour.**

**You will need**

2kg crab apples

1.2 litres of water

450g of preserving sugar (quantity depends on your juice yield)

**Method**

1. Wash and cut up the crab apples. Place them into a jam kettle or large thick bottomed pan.
2. Pour the water over the apples, just enough to cover. Bring them slowly to the boil, turn down the heat and simmer for about 1½ hours. Stir the pan occasionally and with a potato masher break up the fruit to extract the pectin.
3. Ladle the cooked fruit and juice into a scalded jam bag or muslin cloth doubled over and allow the juice to drip through into another pan. This takes all afternoon so please do not watch it!
4. Measure the juice: for each pint of strained juice, you will need 450g of preserving sugar.
5. Stir them together over a low heat until the sugar has dissolved and then bring to the boil. Boiling rapidly until setting point is reached. This takes about 15 minutes.
6. Take the pan off the stove, drain and with a ladle skim the jelly. Ladle into sterilised, warm jars. The jelly will cool and set very quickly. When cold, top the jars with a little greaseproof paper circles and screw on the lids.

**PIP'S TIP**

## Crab Apples

What can I say about crab apples except I got lucky; there was a beautiful tree already in the garden when we moved here. My mother occasionally prunes it in early spring.

# Gooseberry & Elderflower Jam

## *Makes 3 x 500g jars*

**I have used red and green gooseberries here. The red variety are much sweeter than traditional green ones and with the addition of elderflower cordial it just works beautifully.**

**You will need**

600g green gooseberries, top and tailed

400g red gooseberries, top and tailed

150ml water

1kg preserving sugar

20g butter

50ml elderflower cordial

**Method**

1. Place the gooseberries in a large saucepan and cover with the water.
1. Bring the fruit up to a simmer over medium heat, just to soften.
2. Stir in the sugar until dissolved, this will take about 10 minutes.
3. Bring the jam up to boil over a high heat and boil to cook for a further 20 minutes stirring occasionally. Skim off any surfacing impurities and discard.
4. To check the jam will set, pour a little on a cold plate and run your index finger through it. If the jam is ready it will take a few seconds to fill the trace of your finger. If not, it will cover the finger line immediately.
5. If the jam is too thin just continue boiling for a further 10 minutes.
6. When the jam is at the correct consistency remove from the heat and add the elderflower cordial, butter, and stir gently then allow the jam to settle and cool slightly.
7. Pour the jam into sterilised jam jars and cover with greaseproof paper. When the jam is cold seal the jars.

This jam can be used for both sweet and savoury dishes. Great for breakfast on hot buttered toast or lovely with roast belly of pork.

**PIP'S TIP**

### Gooseberries

Pick fully ripened gooseberries carefully as they are very soft and likely to burst between your fingers. In late winter you must remember to feed them. I use chicken manure as fertiliser. I put it in a watering can mix well and pour it around the plant. Excess fruit can be frozen in bags or turned into jam.

### Elderflowers

We have a lot of elderflower trees around the farm. Bees love elderflowers and from May to June they make the most of the pollen. I placed my beehives near the elderflower trees to make life easier for them. As it turns out, the trees act as a protective canopy and windbreak to the hives so it all just naturally makes sense.

# Elderflower cordial

It is the end of May, and the elderflowers are in bloom everywhere including our garden. Make sure you pick the elderflowers on a hot sunny day. This cordial is great for children, they love it mixed with soda water and crushed ice or made into iced lollies. However, if you are a big child like me pour a small amount of cordial into the bottom of a glass and top it up with champagne. It is fabulous.

**You will need**

1½ litres of water boiled and cooled

1.5kg caster sugar

25 elderflower heads (picked on a hot dry day)

50g citric acid (you can get this at the chemist in powder form)

2 lemons, unwaxed

**Method**

1. Boil the water and pour it into a large bowl to cool.
2. When cold stir in the caster sugar and immediately add the freshly picked elderflower heads and stir again.
3. Stir in the citric acid – this acts as a preservative and stops the cordial from fermenting.
4. Cut the lemons into small chunks and add to the bowl.
5. Cover with cling film and refrigerate overnight.
6. Strain the elderflower cordial through a fine muslin cloth or fine tea towel into another bowl. With a ladle pour the cordial into sterilised bottles with stoppers or small plastic containers with lids. It will keep in the fridge for about 3 weeks or you can freeze it in the plastic containers.

Pour a little cordial over some vanilla ice cream with red fruits or when making an apple pie pour a dash over the apples. I like to add some to my apple sauce for roast pork.

# Cucumber Pickle

## *Makes 3 x 400g jars*

Pip planted cucumbers from seed in the greenhouse at the end of March. With the greenhouse being quite small, he had to move the plant outside to the garden to make room for the invading tomatoes. They are a bit bent, a bit short but very long on flavour. To sterilise my pickling jars, I use boiling hot soapy water to wash and rinse before drying on a tray in a medium oven.

**You will need**

3 small or 2 large cucumbers

50g salt

2 large onions, diced

2 cloves of garlic

2 large red chillies, chopped

1 red pepper, diced

375ml cider vinegar

250g soft brown sugar

½ tsp of turmeric

3 cloves crushed

2-3 star anise

1 tbs of mustard seeds

40g cornflour

40g mustard powder

**Method**

1. Top and tail the cucumbers and with a sharp knife and cut them down the middle. With the point of a teaspoon, scrape out the seeds and discard them. Lay the cucumbers down on a tray and sprinkle the insides with salt and leave to marinate. The salt will pull out impurities and the juices from the cucumber keeping it nice and crunchy. Leave it for 10 minutes then wash them off and dry in a clean kitchen towel then dice the cucumber into thin 2cm pieces and place them in a bowl.
2. Put a large pan on the stove half filled with water and bring it to the boil. Dice the onions into 2cm pieces. As the water boils add the onions. Bring them back to the boil and quickly strain them off. Place them in a bowl to cool. Use the same water and repeat this process (blanching) for the red pepper.
3. Cut the chillies in half, deseed, and finely slice them. Sprinkle them over the cucumber. Peel and chop the garlic.

**For the pickling liquor**

1. Pour the vinegar into a large saucepan. Add the dried spices.
2. Add the sugar and cook until the sugar has dissolved. Simmer for 2 minutes.
3. Add the cucumber, chilli, diced onion, and red pepper and bring to the boil. Strain off the vegetables immediately and put them in a sterilised bowl.
4. Return the vinegar to a pan and bring it to the boil.
5. Mix with 2-3 tablespoons of water the cornflower and mustard seed and with a small whisk stir it into the vinegar to thicken. Turn down the heat and cook the liquor for about 10 minutes. Do not let it catch on the bottom.
6. Pour the liquor over the vegetables and mix well. Fill the jars and when cold seal them with greaseproof paper and a lid. Do not open for about a month.

This pickle is great for ham sandwiches or any cold meats. Try it with some pate on toast or with cheese.

# Red Cabbage with Port & Apple

*Serves 6-8*

There is an affinity between sweet red cabbage and game, especially venison. But it can happily make an appearance alongside your Sunday roast, too. For the best result, prepare the night before and store it in a covered bowl in the fridge. All the flavours combine to make a gorgeous, rich tangy dish. Just slowly re-heat in a pan when needed.

**You will need**

1 red cabbage 450-500g, trimmed and finely sliced

½ tsp of powdered clove

½ tsp of grated nutmeg

1 cinnamon stick

4 tbsp red wine vinegar

2-3 jumpier berries

1 orange, zest, and juice but pith removed

1 glass of port

1 garlic clove, peeled and chopped

40g soft brown sugar

250ml apple juice

1 large apple, peeled and sliced

1 large onion, peeled and finely sliced

80g butter

salt and black pepper

**Method**

1. In a large saucepan add the butter, sliced red cabbage, grated nutmeg and sprinkle with the powdered clove and on a medium heat gently cook.
2. Add the cinnamon stick and pour in the red wine vinegar. Crush the juniper berries and add the zest of 1 orange and its juice. Make sure you have removed the white pith from the zest.
3. Add the glass of port and the garlic clove peeled and crushed. Stir.
4. Sprinkle the brown sugar over the cabbage and pour in the apple juice.
5. When the cabbage is slightly tender add the sliced apple and onion. Add the salt and pepper to taste.
6. Now turn down the heat and put a lid on the pan. Cook for 30 minutes but remember to give the cabbage a good stir from time to time.
7. After 30 minutes check to see if the cabbage is tender.
8. Remove the pan from the heat and allow to cool.

When the cabbage is cool enough place in a covered bowl and refrigerate preferably overnight to enhance the flavour. Simply re-heat when required.

**PIP'S TIP**

## Brassicas: Purple Sprouting Broccoli, Cabbage, Savoy

In the summer months the cabbage white butterfly can wreak havoc with your brassicas. I invested in a cloche that will let nothing but water and light through. You just need to lay it over the top of the vegetables to stop caterpillars eating your plants. This is an environmentally friendly alternative to spraying the leaves.

Keep used eggshells, sprinkle the crushed shells around the base of each plant. I also use coffee grounds and ash from the fireplace. Slugs really hate it. I refuse to use slug pellets. When wildlife eats the slugs that have been poisoned, they may die also.

# Cucumber & Mint Raita

## *Serves 6*

This is quite simple to make. The mint in the herb garden seems to double in size every few weeks and yet we still keep a large stone pot of it growing by the back door. It helps when you want to quickly grab a few leaves for your jug of Pimm's.

**You will need**

400ml natural live yoghurt
2 tbsp of mint, finely chopped
1 medium size cucumber, peeled, cut in half length ways, deseeded, and grated
1 tsp sugar
1 garlic clove, peeled and crushed to a paste
salt and milled black pepper
½ tsp of cumin (ground)
1 fresh red chilli, deseeded and finely chopped
½ lime, juice of

**Method**

1. In a large bowl add the prepared cucumber then add all the other ingredients.
2. Gently stir in the yoghurt and mint.
3. Place into a bowl and cover with cling film. Refrigerate until required.

# Glazed Beetroot in Cider Vinegar

## *Serves 12*

Pip planted two rows of beetroot at the beginning of April. With such good soil further enhanced with some well-rotted horse manure, my son produced some of the best beetroot I have seen and tasted.

**You will need**

2kg raw beetroot
180g caster sugar
225ml cider vinegar
225ml water
salt

**Method**

1. Peel and grate half of the raw beetroot and place it in a saucepan. To avoid red-stained hands, wear rubber gloves.
2. Add the sugar, pour on the cider vinegar, and add the water. Bring the mixture to the boil, skim off any impurities with a ladle and simmer gently for half an hour. During this cooking period the beetroot will release all its colour and flavour.
3. Strain the mixture through a fine sieve into a clean pan pushing it down with the back of a ladle to extract all the flavour. Discard the residue from the sieve.
4. Bring the liquor to the boil and reduce the volume by a third until it thickens to a syrupy consistency. If you are not using it immediately, let it cool and pour it into a plastic container and refrigerate when cold.
5. Wash and cook the remaining beetroot in boiling salted water until tender. Drain into a colander and, again with your rubber gloves on, peel while the beetroot is still warm. Slice the beetroot and add it to the beetroot syrup.
6. Take out the amount you need with some syrup and place it in a pan over a high heat for about 5 minutes or until glazed.

# Carrot & Orange Puree

*Serves 4*

**Our carrots went directly into the soil as seeds at the beginning of April. By July we had a considerable crop. Freshly pulled carrots taste sublime and their sweetness, combined with orange, make this dish a simple delight. Especially good with pork.**

**You will need**

6 large carrots, peeled and chopped small

100g butter

1 dstsp sugar

salt and white pepper

2 oranges, juice of

100ml vegetable stock

2 tbsp double cream

**Method**

1. Peel the carrots and cut them into small pieces. Place them in saucepan with the butter and cook until the butter has melted. This takes 2 minutes.
2. Add the sugar, salt and pepper and the orange juice. Bring the mix to the boil and pour in the vegetable stock.
3. Cook the carrots until soft and the liquid has evaporated by at least half of its original volume.
4. Pour the mixture into a liquidiser and blend until smooth. Taste for seasoning and with a spatula spoon the puree into a small saucepan. On a medium heat bring the puree up to temperature but do not boil and gently stir in the double cream. Serve immediately.

For a celeriac puree which is super with game dishes, proceed as for the carrot puree but instead of the orange juice, double the stock i.e. 200ml. If you prefer, use a white chicken stock instead of the vegetable.

**PIP'S TIP**

## Carrots, Swede, and Parsnips

I found out the hard way that carrots do not grow in stony soil. You really need sandy soil so second time around I planted ours in an inch layer of sand with compost on top and a final layer of fine soil. After 21 days my carrots appeared as seedlings and grew long, straight perfectly formed. This applies pretty much to all root vegetables. The sandy soil is suitable for the roots to grown down searching for moisture.

# Rose Hip Syrup

### *3-4 bottles*

From mid-September onwards, you can see the rose hip in the hedgerow. We tend to pick them on a dry day and preferably after a frost when the skins are soft. Rose hips are terribly good for you and contain a huge amount of vitamin C. Three rose hips contain more vitamin C than an orange, I am told. Pour it on ice cream, rice pudding, panna cotta or even into porridge and yoghurt. Not wanting to exaggerate, but rose hip jelly with blue cheeses or cold meats is mind-blowing.

**You will need**

1kg rose hips

3 litres of water

500g golden caster sugar

**Method**

1. Top and tail the rose hips and chop them in half.
2. Place a pan on the stove with two litres of water and bring it to the boil. Add the Rose hips and bring them back to the boil. Take the pan off the stove and allow the fruit to infuse for about 20 minutes.
3. Using a ladle pour the rose hip liquid into a muslin cloth, doubled over a sieve or colander standing over another saucepan to catch the dripping liquid.
4. Return all the drained pulp to the saucepan and add the remaining 1 litre of water. Bring back to the boil and infuse again to extract the maximum amount of flavour. Pour the juice into a clean muslin cloth as before and simmer on the stove until it measures about 1 litre.
5. Add the sugar and keep stirring until dissolved. Bring the syrup back to the boil and cook for a further 5 minutes.
6. Pour the syrup into warm clean bottles about 25cm from the top. If you are using cork stoppers push them into the tops of the bottles to seal but not all the way down. It is imperative that your bottles and lids are completely sterilised and dry before use.
7. Place the bottles into a deep saucepan or jam kettle filled with cold water and bring it slowly to the boil. Simmer for five minutes. Remove the bottles, push down the stoppers and wipe the bottles dry and store.

**PIP'S TIP**

## Rose hips

Rose hips are the seed pods of roses and grow in the hedgerows in the autumn. They are very good for you and contain lots of vitamin C. Dad likes to make his Rose Hip Syrup to keep us healthy.

# Damson Gin

**This is one of Suzi's favourite homemade tipples. In the cold winter months it is her seasonal drink of choice, tasting all the better for the fruit coming from our own tree. This recipe works for other fruits such as raspberries, blackberries and of course sloes.**

**You will need**

600g of damsons pricked

600g of undyed caster sugar

1 (75cl) bottle of gin

1 vanilla pod, split (optional)

**Method**

1. Wash and dry the damsons. I like to prick the damsons with a skewer to release the juice, but it is purely optional. Do not use any damaged or bruised fruit.
2. Once all the fruit is prepared place it in a large jar and cover with the sugar and pour in the gin.
3. Stir it occasionally for the first couple of weeks, then leave it alone.

For the best results you should leave it for at least 3 months but the longer you keep it the better it gets. We do have one bottle from 2017 but that is a rarity and the others seem to mysteriously disappear!

**PIP'S TIP**

## Damsons & Sloes

My mother loves flavoured gin so we pick damsons and sloes after the first frosts when their skins are thin and break down without you having to take the trouble to prick them with a pin to release the juice. Another method we use is to put them in a freezer overnight and the skins will burst for you.

# Walnut Dressing for Salads

### *Makes 200ml*

**Nut dressings are great to add a different flavour to your salads. Nut oil is strong so I dilute it fairly heavily with another oil like groundnut or sunflower. This recipe also works for a hazelnut version – just substitute the base oil.**

**You will need**

1 garlic clove, crushed and peeled

salt and milled black pepper, to taste

1 tsp caster sugar

50ml sherry vinegar

100ml groundnut oil

100ml walnut oil

**Method**

Mix all the ingredients together and decant into a bottle or Kilner jar with a tight-fitting lid. It will keep for weeks.

For a quick salad try some mixed leaves washed and dried on a clean kitchen towel. I use baby dandelion leaves, little gem hearts and frisee lettuce. Bind with a little dressing, crumble some blue cheese, toasted walnuts, and some little garlic croutons. For sweetness try some dried cherries.

# Classic French Dressing

### *Serves 4*

**You will need**

1 tsp Dijon mustard

1tsp white wine vinegar

½ tsp sugar

salt and milled black pepper

4 tbsp olive oil

½ clove garlic, peeled and sliced in half

1 sprig of tarragon

**Method**

1. In a bowl mix all the ingredients together with a whisk until combined.
2. Pour the dressing into a jar and seal until needed.

# Parsley, Spinach & Watercress Sauce

### *Serves 4*

**You will need**

1 bunch parsley, washed and picked

1 bunch young spinach leaves, picked

1 bunch watercress, picked

1 small bunch sorrel or some basil leaves

200ml mayonnaise (recipe on p23)

100ml double cream, whipped

¼ lemon, juice of

salt and white pepper

**Method**

1. Place a large pan ½ filled with water on the stove to boil. When boiling first add the parsley, this takes longer to cook. After 2 minutes add the remaining herbs and blanch them for 1 minute.
2. Strain the herbs through a sieve and immediately cool them down in iced cold water. Strain again and squeeze them into a ball. Squeeze out as much water as you can.
3. Finely chop the herbs and add them to the bowl.
4. Mix the herbs with the mayonnaise.
5. Lightly whip the cream and fold it into the sauce.
6. Season with salt and white pepper, a little lemon juice to taste. Transfer to a serving bowl.

This sauce is fabulous with all fried fish. Try it with tempura squid or tempura prawns and of course sole.

# Herb Butter

**Pip's herb garden has chives, thyme, coriander, plus flat leaf and curly parsley. It exploded in to life in the warm spring weather. All of them are great for making a herb butter with the exception of thyme, as it is rather coarse. This compound butter can be stored in the freezer wrapped in greaseproof paper. Use it to put under the skin of a chicken for roasting. Or to top a piece of fish at the end of grilling. Stir into soups, especially a vegetable broth, or to thicken a sauce for fish.**

**You will need**

1kg unsalted butter
1 large bunch flat leaf parsley
1 large bunch curly parsley
1 large bunch chives
1 small bunch coriander
1 lemon, juice of
2-3 drops of Tabasco
2-3 drops Worcestershire sauce
2 fresh red chilies, deseeded and finely chopped
3 garlic cloves, chopped to a paste
salt to taste

**Method**

1. Chop the butter into a mixing bowl and allow to soften. Whisk with an electric mixer until it turns white.
2. Wash, pick, dry and finely chop the parsley.
3. Chop a little coriander – not too much as it is strong and will overpower the flavour of the other ingredients.
4. Put a saucepan of water on the stove to boil add the chives and immediately take them out and place them into a bowl of iced water. This will soften them and stops them from oxidising in the butter. Strain the chives through a sieve and press them dry between two clean tea towels, removing as much water as possible. Chop and add them to the chopped parsley.
5. Put all the herbs into the whipped butter. Add the lemon juice, Tabasco, Worcestershire sauce, garlic and chilli. Season with a little salt.
6. Mix the herbs into the butter. This amount should make 4 rolls.
7. Layout a sheet of greaseproof paper on a work surface. With a spatula take out a quarter of the herb butter and place it in a line ¼ way up the paper. Fold the paper over the butter and mould it into a sausage shape. Roll it like you would a rolling pin and seal the ends turning the paper all the time. Place the butter on a tray. Repeat this process for all the remaining butter.
8. Use some immediately or store in the freezer until needed.

Cut off a piece each time you need some. Remember to seal the end with a little cling film and return it to the freezer for the next time.

This herb butter can be used for several dishes and you have the use of fresh herbs all year round.

**PIP'S TIP**

## Protecting Beehives

Wasps are the bee's enemy at large. Wasps kill for honey. Recycle an empty jam jar, half filled with a mix of jam, sugar, and water, cover the top with foil and make some holes large enough for the wasps to enter. They will make a 'beeline' for the super sweet syrup. I recommend placing the jar about two metres away from the hive. When we eat outdoors wasps can be very annoying, so we place a jar at the end of the table to keep them away.

The more sun you have on the hives during the day, the more the bees will be out flying and that means more honey. In winter, you need a strong windbreak as you do not want them toppling over. I always put a big heavy rock or some support on the lid, so it does not get blown away. We learned this during Storm Francis.